A Cruising Guide
to New Jersey Waters

A Cruising Guide to New Jersey Waters

Captain Donald Launer

Rutgers University Press

New Brunswick, New Jersey

Library of Congress Cataloging-in-Publication Data

Launer, Donald, 1926–
  A cruising guide to New Jersey waters / Donald Launer.
    p.   cm.
  Includes bibliographical references and index.
  ISBN 0-8135-2238-2 (alk. paper)
  1. Boats and boating—New Jersey—Guidebooks.   2. Waterways—New
Jersey—Guidebooks.   3. New Jersey—Guidebooks.   I. Title.
GV776.N5L38   1995
796.1'09749—dc20   95-8590
                                                                 CIP

British Cataloging-in-Publication information available

Published by Rutgers University Press, New Brunswick, New Jersey
Manufactured in the United States of America

Affectionately dedicated to my wife, Elsie,
our children, Kathy and Tom,
and our grandchildren, Jennifer and Nancy
—outstanding crew members all

⚓ Contents

⚓ ⚓

⚓ List of Illustrations and Tables

Photographs

⚓ ⚓

$\mathcal{C}$harts

*T*ables

⚓ Acknowledgments

*A*ny book such as this is a compilation of facts from many sources: local watermen, history books, government publications, and, primarily, my own cruising experiences. I have been fortunate to have had the enthusiastic cooperation of many people and organizations in this endeavor. A few I would like to give credit to are Marion Figley, editor in chief of *The Beachcomber* and writer for the *Sandpaper*, for her editorial suggestions and review; John Smath of Lanoka Harbor, who shared his expertise and experience from a lifetime on Raritan Bay and its tributaries; Andrew Willner, New Jersey/New York Baykeeper, who provided insights on Sandy Hook Bay, Raritan Bay, Arthur Kill, Kill Van Kull, and Newark Bay as I cruised these waters with him; Cynthia Poten, Delaware Riverkeeper; and Captain Nicholas Prahl, chief of the mapping and charting branch of NOAA. In this book I have used excerpts from some of the articles that I have written for *Offshore*, the northeast boating magazine, with the blessing of Herb Gliick, publisher.

Most of the photographs are my own. Keith Hamilton, of Studio-9 in Waretown, provided the aerial photographs, which provide striking views of our shoreline. He has been involved with the preparation and darkroom work necessary for the final presentation. Other photographs are from Bill Schultz, baykeeper auxiliary; Linda Riley of the Camden Aquarium; The Port Imperial Marina in Weehawkin; and Trump's Castle Associates.

The nautical charts are reproduced through the courtesy of the NOAA's National Ocean Service, a branch of the Department of Commerce.

If I have left anyone out, they are no less appreciated.

A Cruising Guide
to New Jersey Waters

Introduction

*T*he fascination associated with traveling near or on the water seems to be imprinted on the human soul. Is it because we came from the sea and water still comprises most of our physical being, or is it because we know inherently that without water we couldn't exist? As small children we were drawn to streams, rivers, lakes, and oceans; and as adults we can still sit by the hour, watching the breaking surf, a cascading waterfall, or a brook flowing through the woods. This appeal transcends our practical facade and touches our most romantic instincts. It manifests itself in the need to become a part of our environment, to be on or near the water, and to experience our most primal feelings.

For many people this translates into the desire to skipper their own boats—to replicate in some small way the voyages of their ancestors and to feel at one with the waters that comprise most of the surface of our planet.

This book, then, is a cruising guide designed to entice recreational boat owners in the northeast, whether of power or sail boats, to explore the navigable waters at their doorstep. It will also provide the armchair sailor with an opportunity to vicariously cruise the waters that border and lie within the Garden State. Included in the guide is information on navigation, anchorages, marinas, and weather, along with shoreside activities (such as waterside restaurants, sightseeing, historic locations, nature preserves, and entertainment), as well as safety tips—the type of information that is not available through government publications. Maritime adventures from the past are also chronicled for each area, so we will be cruising through history as well as through geography.

When I say the book deals with the "navigable" waters of New Jersey, I use the term in both the legal and the more pragmatic sense—that is, those waters subject to tidal flow that are actually navigable. Although I have also spent thousands of hours on the nonnavigable waters of New Jersey in both my kayak and canoe (enjoying every moment), this cruising guide will limit itself to ocean and tidewater cruising.

With the exception of the fifty-three-mile-long New York State land boundary on the north, New Jersey is almost completely surrounded by water, and a small boat can cruise more than three hundred miles around the navigable perimeter of the state. The western boundary is the Delaware River, which is used recreationally by small boats along its entire length. It is only navigable below the falls at Trenton, and our trip up the Delaware will stop there.

Where I have named marinas or restaurants, it is because they are representative of the area. No endorsement is intended, and no inference should be made about those not mentioned. There will undoubtedly be readers who take exception to some of the ideas expressed—it has always been so. Herman Melville, when counseling a young American writer, lamented: "Pierre, . . . it is impossible to talk or to write, without throwing oneself helplessly open to criticism."

The material contained in the book is, however, to the best of my knowledge and at the time of writing, as accurate as possible, taking into account that our shoreline is constantly changing and that facilities on shore (marinas, restaurants, prices, and the like) are also open to change. Even as this book goes to press, I continue to explore in my auxiliary schooner *Delphinus*, in my Boston whaler, and sometimes in my kayak. When new things are discovered, or errors are brought to light, they will, along with input from readers, contribute to better coverage in future editions.

Please note that the charts reproduced in this book are not intended to take the place of up-to-date NOAA government charts, tide tables, the *U.S. Coast Pilot*, or proper navigational practices. Indeed, we have made no attempt to reproduce the high level of detail in the original charts and have used the charts primarily to show the relationship between different waterways and land masses. The author and the publisher disclaim any liability for loss or damage to persons or property that may occur as a result of the use or interpretation of any information in this book.

Where there is a subjective opinion expressed, whether positive or negative, it is strictly my own. Those enamored with Atlantic City might be bored spending a day treading for clams, and vice-versa. Everyone's preferences and ideas are different, but New Jersey's waters offer a diversity that should satisfy all. My own views come from paddling, rowing, sailing, motoring, and swimming in New Jersey waters, a vocation as well as an avocation that continues nearly every day during the boating season.

Finally, I am not as interested in showing how the greatest distance can be covered in the least amount of time, but rather in the quality and safety of a life

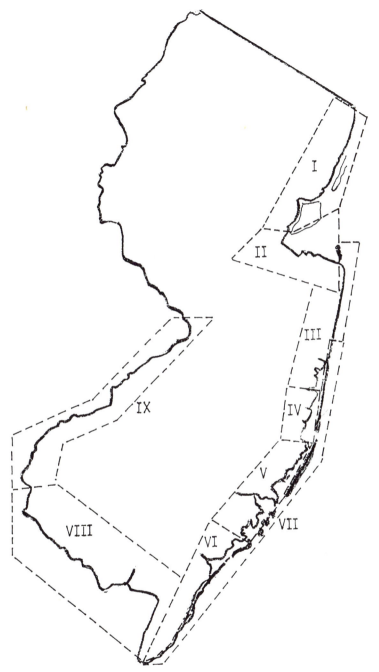

$\mathcal{C}$hart 1.1 Outline of New Jersey, indicating the areas covered by each of the 9 chapters

afloat. The enjoyment of being on board, savoring the delights of a cruising vacation in a safe manner, is my primary concern—those in a hurry should take a car or a plane.

We will begin our cruise at the northern limit of New Jersey's navigable waters, the Hudson River at the New Jersey–New York border, and follow the river south through New York Harbor, the Upper and Lower bays, and the Kill Van Kull and Arthur Kill between New Jersey and Staten Island.

We'll then explore Raritan Bay and Sandy Hook Bay, which are enclosed by Sandy Hook, the Atlantic Highlands, and Staten Island. While there, we will look at the many tributaries that enter the bay from the south and west.

From Sandy Hook our cruise will take us south along the Atlantic coast to Manasquan Inlet, where the option of an inland passage becomes available. In separate chapters we'll take the offshore passage south as well as the inland route to Cape May.

The cruise through Delaware Bay, with side trips to the little rivers on the north, takes us to the Delaware River, where our course follows the river to the head of navigation at Trenton (chart 1.1).

At the end of most chapters there is a mileage table, showing distances in statute miles between locations mentioned in the text. In chapters 4, 5, and 6,

The author sailing his schooner, *Delphinus*, on Barnegat Bay

which cover the intracoastal route, no mileage tables are provided since distances along this intracoastal route are clearly marked on the charts.

I have been sailing New Jersey's waters for more than sixty years and hope to continue doing so for many more. Thus, the recipe in this book includes a large measure of practical experience gained throughout a lifetime mixed with research and a dash of information garnered from those who have made a life on the water either of work or of play.

It is unfortunately common for the older generation, when recalling time spent on our waters in their youth, to lament for yesteryear—for lost places, people, and lifestyles. Everyone likes to believe that his or her childhood belonged to a larger age of innocence, a time that no one will ever see again. But it is a form of conceit to believe that the golden age of New Jersey's waters exists in memory and that within our lifetime (due to industrial, social, and bureaucratic upheaval), our waters have fallen from grace. It's a nostalgia ill-used. Better to approach a day on the water with wide-eyed wonder and the heart of a child.

I'm sure many New Jersey as well as out-of-state mariners view cruising New Jersey waters as an uninteresting prospect. To them I say, "Read on"; and to those approaching my vintage, my recommendation is: "Sail before sunset!"

Chapter One

The Hudson River at the New Jersey/New York State Line to New York's Lower Bay

*O*ur cruise of New Jersey's navigable waters begins on the north-eastern corner of the state, the Hudson River at the New Jersey–New York State line. At this point, directly across the Hudson from Hastings-on-Hudson in Westchester, New York, the state line extends to midriver.

It is 315 miles from the Hudson's source in the Adirondack Mountains of upstate New York to its mouth in New York Harbor between the Battery and Jersey City, and the river is navigable as far north as Troy. For most of its length, the Hudson River is entirely within New York State, but for the last 16 miles, until it merges with New York Harbor, the river shares its banks and waters with New Jersey.

From the headwaters of time, the Hudson has always held an attraction for the early inhabitants of North America, and radio carbon dating shows that humans lived in the Hudson River valley back at least as far as 4000 B.C.

As we travel south on the broad river from the New York border, we see to our west the soaring cliffs of the majestic Palisades, which rise up from the New Jersey shoreline and extend from just north of the New Jersey–New York bor-der to a point near the borders of Bergen and Hudson counties. The Palisades were created 190 million years ago, when molten basalt erupted through the sandstone mantle and cooled into vertical columns that resemble the logs used to build traditional fortifications. The early pioneers dubbed them by the same name—palisades. We are fortunate that they have been preserved in their natu-ral state by the Palisades Interstate Park Commission. In New Jersey, the Pal-isades Park runs for 10 miles, from the New York State line to a point just below the George Washington Bridge.

Wind patterns on the river are largely determined by the hills of the Pal-

The New Jersey Palisades along the Hudson River near Alpine. Armstrong's experimental FM tower rises above the trees.

isades at the southern end and by the mountains on each bank further north, which channel the wind so that it travels along the axis of the river, blowing from either the north or south. Thus, cruising sailboats are usually either on a run or are propelled by their so-called iron wind. Those under sail who try tacking into an opposing wind and tide find this usually results in little or no net gain.

Few hazards exist for the small boat skipper on this stretch of the Hudson. Tides run about two knots at their peak, and there is ample water depth; mid-channel is about forty feet. One must, however, be alert to debris in the water and to traffic, including large ships, tugs, barges, and ferries. It's wise to give large ships, and especially tugboats with tows, the right of way without question; if there is any concern about their intentions they should be contacted on VHF Ch-13. Keep in mind that stopping or turning a large ship can take a mile or more to accomplish, and small craft close under its bow are obscured from view. When a small boat in the vicinity of a large ship plans a change in direction, the move should be decisive, almost exaggerated, so there is no question about the course change or intention.

The waters of the Hudson River are making a substantial recovery from the major pollution problems of the 1950s. At that time manufacturing plants along its banks dumped waste chemicals into the water, and cities used it as a disposal site for raw sewage, more than 300 million gallons every day from New York City alone. Professional seafarers termed New York Harbor a "clean port," not because of the water purity; but rather because wood-boring worms, teredos, which destroy wooden ships, barges, and piers, were unable to thrive in the polluted waters. Finally, public awareness of the ever-increasing problem caused activism to replace complacency, and the federal, state, and city governments were prompted to adopt stringent environmental regulations. These new regulations and substantial penalties for failure to comply with them (along with watchdog citizen-advocacy groups on behalf of a clean environment), have made a noticeable change in the Hudson's waters, which are returning year by year from a legacy of environmental abuse.

Despite the Hudson's environmental problems, it is the only river in the eastern United States that still has the same aquatic wildlife as it did when the east coast was first colonized by Europeans.

As we travel south along the New Jersey Palisades, we come to the first New Jersey marina at Alpine, nestled on a short skirt of land between the river and the foot of the cliffs. The Alpine Boat Basin is located about three and a half miles south of the New York border and is operated by the Palisades Interstate Park Commission. It has slips with electricity and water that are sheltered from the wash of Hudson River traffic, a gas dock, and picnic facilities. Before the Tappan Zee Bridge was built in 1955, a ferry service carried cars between this spot and Yonkers on the New York side. It was the only way across the river between the George Washington Bridge and Bear Mountain. At the Alpine Marina there are two picturesque walking paths along the Hudson. Both the Shore Path at the base of the Palisades next to the river and the Long Path, which runs along the top of the cliffs, provide the walker or jogger with a spectacular setting.

South of Alpine a road called River Drive has been hewn into the face of the mountain. Trees arch across the road overhead; little brooks tumble down the face of the cliffs; and magnificent views of the river can be seen through breaks in the trees. It's a delightful lane for a drive, a hike, or a bike ride (provided the bike has low gears).

At the top of the Palisades, at Alpine, a large tower with two horizontal crossarms is easily seen for miles around. It is historically important in the field of broadcasting. In 1935, E. H. Armstrong, in a famous paper presented at the Institute of Radio Engineers, presented his invention of FM (frequency modulation), and his first experiments in FM broadcasting were performed at this location.

Two miles before the George Washington Bridge, which links New Jersey and Manhattan Island, one will find the Englewood Boat Basin, located on a narrow strip of land at the base of the Palisades. From the river, the sailboats' masts in the marina look like mere toothpicks against the lofty cliffs. The marina has protected slips and a fuel dock and is also operated by the park commission. Shore Path, along the Palisades, leads from this marina to the Alpine Marina and beyond. The Englewood Boat Basin is located directly across the river from the Spuyten Duyvil Creek, which separates the north end of Manhattan Island from the Bronx (the Bronx is named for Bronck's Farm, owned by Jonas Bronck, who farmed 500 acres there).

Few services currently exist for the small boat along Manhattan's waterfront. By contrast, every year there are more and more marinas and small craft facilities being built along the river on the opposite shore in New Jersey. Unfortunately, the dream of creating a Gold Coast along the New Jersey waterfront across from Manhattan that took shape in the 1980s, never quite lived up to its promise. (When the 1987 stock-market crash sent Manhattan property values and rents tumbling, many New York firms that had originally planned to move across the river reevaluated their options.) Now, slowly, empty office space is being filled, but many of the decaying piers that were originally slated for demolition and reconstruction have remained untouched.

On the Hudson River, looking south toward the George Washington Bridge and Manhattan Island

Below the George Washington Bridge, which was completed in the depression year of 1931, the aura of being in a big city takes over, and the hustle and bustle on the water becomes more intense. On one side of the river are the natural cliffs of the New Jersey Palisades, on the other the artificial cliffs of Manhattan. There are two marinas in the New Jersey town of Edgewater, between the bridge and the ferryboat restaurant *Binghamton*. Although it would be nice, there is no tie-up at the restaurant.

Manhattan, from this vantage point, puts on a benign face and seems to be the Emerald City of Oz—without dirt, crime, or traffic jams. The concrete monoliths create an incomparable panorama, and all lines in our view seem to be vertical, buildings reaching skyward.

As we follow the surge of the tide past Manhattan, we see that the New Jersey shoreline across the river is being revitalized with marinas, luxury apartments, and town houses. Typical of this rebirth are two marinas in Weehawken. (History buffs will remember that Weehawken was the site of the famous duel between Alexander Hamilton and Aaron Burr, in which Hamilton was mortally wounded.) The name Weehawken is an American Indian name, meaning "rows of trees"; it referred to the vertical rock columns of the Palisades that resembled the edge of a forest.

The marinas in Weehawken give easy access to midtown Manhattan. One is called Lincoln Harbor Yacht Club. Its name may be misleading since it is not strictly a yacht club—it is not a membership club and does not offer reciprocal privileges to members of other yacht clubs—and it welcomes transients. It has a country-club atmosphere, with restaurants, exercise rooms, and dock stewards. From here it's a short trip into Manhattan by car, bus, ferry, or PATH train. The marina can be contacted on VHF Ch-16.

The 350-acre Port Imperial Marina, also in Weehawken, is a full-service marina, offering facilities for transients, fuel, boat repairs, a ship's store, hauling and engine parts, a restaurant, and the FerryBus to Manhattan. Call on VHF Ch-9, Ch-16, or Ch-88A. The marina advertises: "Just 5 blocks and a ferry ride from your favorite Broadway show." Arthur's Landing Restaurant, located there, offers a pretheater dining package that includes a complimentary round-trip ferry service and connecting shuttle bus to and from the New York City theater district.

Along Manhattan's Hudson River waterfront (between 17th and 23rd streets in the Chelsea district and south of where the World War II aircraft carrier *Intrepid* is berthed), The Chelsea Piers project is underway on four 600-foot piers, opening more than a mile of Manhattan's waterfront to a whole range of recreational options. The piers and terminal buildings, built for passenger liner traffic in 1910, will include a marina with slips for recreational boats; Great Hudson's

In Weehawken, looking across the Hudson at the Empire State Building in Manhattan, with Port Imperial Marina in the foreground (photo courtesy of J. B. Grant and Port Imperial Marina)

Sailing School, with instruction, charters, and boat rentals; the Maritime Workshop, which will teach boat building and maintenance skills; an ice-skating rink; and a health club. The organizers hope that some of the facilities will be open for business in 1995.

In Jersey City, directly across the Hudson from the Battery, at the southern tip of Manhattan Island, one will find the relatively new Newport Marina. It is part of the $10 billion dollar Newport community, which, in addition to the marina, includes luxury apartments, a shopping center, theaters, restaurants, and sports facilities, with Manhattan just minutes away by car or subway. It can be contacted on VHF Ch-16.

Whenever I pass lower Manhattan by boat, I recall my father telling me of his first visit to New York City as a child in the late 1890s. In those days the soaring bowsprits of great sailing vessels from all over the world thrust across the crowded waterfront. The forest of masts, the rigging whistling in the wind, and the noise of dock-carts rattling over the cobblestones has now been replaced with the sound of cars and sirens from the express highway that runs beside the river.

The Port of New York handled more tonnage than any other port in the world until 1960. Now, most of the piers on the Hudson along Manhattan Island have fallen into disrepair, while the major shipping vessels—tankers, freighters, and container ships—have moved their base of operation to the New Jersey ports off Newark Bay, like Port Newark and Port Elizabeth, or to those along the Arthur Kill, which separates New Jersey and Staten Island.

During the 1800s, Hoboken, across the river from lower Manhattan, was a vacation spot for New Yorkers, who went there on weekends and holidays, considering it a visit to the country. The short ferry ride took them to the Elysian Fields in Hoboken (then a bucolic setting with woods and rolling lawns), where the adults could spend the day relaxing under the trees while the children frolicked until the picnic lunch was ready. It was here that a diamond was set up on the grass and the first modern baseball game was played in 1845.

South of Jersey City, we enter Upper New York Bay, which is bounded by Manhattan on the north, New Jersey on the west, Brooklyn on the east, and Staten Island and The Narrows to the south (chart 1.2). When we cruise through the harbor, I always keep a sharp lookout for debris in the water, large-ship traffic, and the ferries that charge back and forth from Manhattan to Staten Island, Liberty Island, Governor's Island, Ellis Island, and Jersey City. I never make any naive or theoretical assumptions about who has the right of way—I assume that they do.

Legendary Ellis Island, with its Moorish architecture, is just a few hundred yards off the New Jersey shore and connected to it by a bridge that can only be used by park rangers and employees. This bridge also supplies utilities to the island. The island can be passed within a hundred yards on the eastern side for a better view—but watch out for ferries entering or leaving.

By now, as we skirt the shore of Ellis Island, all eyes on board are directed toward the Statue of Liberty, three-quarters of a nautical mile to our south on Liberty Island, and we wish we had more than one pair of binoculars. The 305-foot monument, which faces southeast to welcome those entering the harbor through The Narrows, was completely refurbished in 1986 and now looks pristine. There are submerged rocks and pilings close to the shore at the north, east, and south sides of the island, but small boats can safely pass within a couple of hundred yards to the east. Again, be sure to keep a watchful eye out for ferry traffic. Landing on shore is prohibited. The only access to the island is by way of the Circle-Line ferries that leave either from lower Manhattan; from New Jersey's Liberty State Park, 600 yards to the west; or from Hoboken. These ferries bring throngs of visitors, over a million a year, to the island.

In 1991 Congress authorized the construction of a footbridge linking Ellis Island and Liberty Island so that visitors would have easy access between these

$\mathcal{C}$hart 1.2 New York Harbor (reproduced from NOAA's Chart #12327)

The Statue of Liberty in New York Harbor

two historical sites. Endless delays have pushed the start date for this project to September 1996, and bureaucracy will probably delay it longer.

We occasionally see some buoys in the water near Liberty Island that look just like lobster-pot buoys, and that's because they are. Lobsters are being caught here, a tangible testament to the improving water quality.

Luckily we haven't forgotten to bring cameras along, since the sights in all directions from this vantage point are spectacular. We now turn east across New York Harbor toward the southern tip of Manhattan, which brings us to the confluence of the East River and the Hudson River at the Battery. (The Battery was named for the battery of ninety-two cannon that the British placed there in 1693 to defend against French attacks.) The twin towers of the World Trade Center are just to the north along the Hudson, and along the Manhattan shoreline of the East River is the picturesque South Street Seaport, with the spider-web cables of the Brooklyn Bridge just beyond.

At the South Street Seaport docks, which are just south of the historic Brooklyn Bridge and next to the Manhattan Yacht Club, one will find the *Wavertree*, a three-masted ship built in 1885; the 1911 four-masted barque *Peking*; the first Ambrose lightship, built in 1908; a 1930 wooden tugboat, the *Lettie G. Howard*; a restored oysterer; and the 1885 cargo schooner *Pioneer*, which takes passengers on daily trips around the harbor.

South Street Seaport

The Brooklyn Bridge

The preservation, restoration, and development of South Street Seaport began, uncertainly, in 1967. (Finally, the Rouse Company, whose wizardry was responsible for Baltimore's Inner Harbor and for Boston's Quincy Market, provided the needed impetus.) South Street, named because this part of Manhattan faces due south, now provides a mosaic of diversions. There are dockside concerts, street musicians and jugglers, shops, restaurants, bookstores, and the nautical cornucopia called Captain Hook's, where two floors of maritime miscellany are sold by a staff dressed as seafarers of the 1700s.

When we leave the East River, heading across the harbor toward the Verrazano Bridge, we usually take the channel between Governors Island and Brooklyn; there is less traffic there and the route is slightly shorter. Governors Island is home to the U.S. Coast Guard, and recreational boats are prohibited from landing there.

The Verrazano Bridge joins the boroughs of Brooklyn and Staten Island and vaults across the hourglass waist of The Narrows, which separates New York's upper and lower bays. The Lower Bay, to the south of The Narrows, is part of the larger bay, which is also comprised of Sandy Hook Bay and Raritan Bay. These are not separate bays, as such, but actually sections of the same body of water, joined by indefinite boundaries. Sandy Hook Bay is the area to the southeast of the Lower Bay, and Raritan Bay is the area to the southwest.

On the north side of Staten Island, as we head south toward the Verrazano, the Kill Van Kull branches off the harbor to the west. This waterway, which is a boundary between New Jersey and Staten Island, New York, connects with the Arthur Kill and is an optional route to Raritan Bay. It also provides an entrance into Newark Bay, and ultimately the Passaic and Hackensack rivers that flow north into the northern New Jersey suburbs. (This alternate route will be discussed later in this chapter.)

When heading through The Narrows, one can encounter an annoying sea that can develop against an opposing wind and tide. In addition, the steel framework of the Verrazano Bridge (as with most large bridges) can affect the compass or cause a course change when a boat is under autopilot. Also, water boundary layers of temperature called thermoclines below the boat can cause the depth-sounder to show only a few feet; but be assured, the depth is more than adequate.

The graceful Verrazano Narrows Bridge is nearly a mile long and is the longest suspension bridge in the world. A civil engineer once told me that the towers of the Verrazano Bridge are vertical, but they're not parallel. As I was pondering this, he explained, "Since the support towers are so far apart, there's a slight curvature of the earth between them."

The Verrazano Bridge across The Narrows was named after the first European explorer to discover and record the existence of this estuary. Approximately seventy-five years after Columbus tried to reach Cathay by sailing west, Florentine navigator Giovanni da Verrazano made another attempt farther north on the American continent, sailing under the French flag. He first sighted the coast near Cape Fear, North Carolina. He headed south for a while but, nervous about the potential threat from Spanish ships, decided to explore north along the coast. Inexplicably, he entirely missed the vast entrances to the Chesapeake and Delaware bays, finally dropping anchor in Sandy Hook Bay. Due to contrary winds and tides, as well as the uncertainty of depths, the ship's boat was rowed up through The Narrows on an exploration of New York Harbor and the lower Hudson River. Verrazano then returned to France without ever giving a name to either the bay or the river.

It wasn't until 1609 that the Hudson River was given the name it currently holds. In September of that year, Henry Hudson's clumsy little Dutch craft *De Halve Maen*, or *The Half Moon*, with a favoring breeze, began a three-week exploration of the river north of The Narrows. After crossing the Upper Bay *The Half Moon* passed an island of rocky hills and forests, where tangled vines clung to the trees and wolves and deer moved through the underbrush. The Canarsie Indian tribe's name for this island was Manna-hatin. By the time Hudson's ship reached the navigable limits of the Hudson, 150 miles from the ocean, it had finally become apparent that this was not the northwest passage to Cathay, but only a river, and they turned southward again from Castle Island, near the present city of Albany. As the Native Americans along the shore watched the ship, like a huge bird with white wings, sail up the river, they surely didn't realize that their lives were about to change forever.

Navigation from the Verrazano, across the bay to the New Jersey shoreline, as well as trips up the tidal tributaries of Sandy Hook Bay and Raritan Bay are explored in Chapter II, but first let's look at that alternate route from New York Harbor to Raritan Bay, the Kill Van Kull, and Arthur Kill.

*T*he Kill Van Kull and Arthur Kill separate Staten Island from New Jersey. Staten Island is a corruption of the original Dutch name *Staaten Eylandt*, named for the States General at that time. In the 1600s both New York and New Jersey claimed Staten Island as their own. To settle the dispute it was finally agreed that New York could have all of the islands in the harbor that could be circumnavigated within twenty-four hours. New Jersey was sure to obtain Staten Island since sailboats of that era had trouble going to windward and sailing through the narrow Kills around Staten Island within twenty-four hours. New York gave Captain Charles Billop and his sloop *Bently* the task. By today's standards the *Bently* looked like an awkward and inefficient little craft; but, through skillful short-tacking and playing the tides, Captain Billop accomplished the impossible, and the Borough of Richmond (Staten Island) became a part of New York City.

Captain Billop was rewarded with lands and a manor house at Tottenville on the island he won for New York. More than one hundred years later his home, which was built in 1668, again found a niche in history when it became the site of the first peace negotiations that led to the end of the American Revolution.

The Kill Van Kull takes the nautical nomad to the industrial waterways of New Jersey seldom visited by recreational boaters, but this doesn't mean the trip is hazardous or devoid of interest. The Kill Van Kull and northern Arthur Kill are the major channels for bulk, containerized, and petroleum cargo in New York Harbor. So, we'll be sharing the traffic lanes with ships that are constricted to the channel and are unable to stop or turn easily; it's our responsibility to stay out of the way. Although these waters have long been avoided by the recreational boater due to debris and pollution, the stringent enforcement of environmental regulations has rendered the water quality probably better than it has been at any time in the last fifty years. Many of the manufacturing and petroleum plants that found an economic advantage in dumping their waste products in these waters have closed down or moved, and the present industries along the water-front have been obliged to reduce their pollution to nearly zero.

When heading west up the Kill Van Kull from New York Harbor, Bayonne, New Jersey, is on our north and Staten Island is to our south (chart 1.3). They are joined by the Bayonne Bridge. With a span of 1,652 feet, it is the longest steel archbridge in the world. Immediately past this bridge, the waterway separates. The channel to the north leads into Newark Bay, which is the route of container ships that use the docks at Port Elizabeth and Port Newark.

Surprisingly, Newark Bay, long a victim of pollution and overindustrialization, supports a large population of blue-claw crab, clams, and fish. The blue crabs are some of the biggest on the eastern seaboard (perhaps because catching them is prohibited), and recently when the Marine Fisheries put in a net for a striped bass survey, the net was so heavy with bass it couldn't be hoisted on board.

At the north end of Newark Bay, beyond the highway fixed bridge and the Conrail lift bridge, one comes to the confluence of the Passaic River and the Hackensack River. The Passaic River, the second longest river within New Jersey (next to the Raritan), has its origins in the Great Swamp. It is navigable by small boat all the way to the town of Passaic, although crossed by numerous fixed, swing, lift, and bascule bridges. In 1881, one of the first successful submarines was launched into the Passaic at Paterson by its inventor, John Holland. Surprisingly, a hundred years ago the Passaic River was also an important link in freight commerce between New York City and Pennsylvania.

America was canal crazy in the 1800s. In the northeast alone, more than four thousand miles of canals were built. When a link from New York City to the coal- and iron-producing areas of eastern Pennsylvania was proposed, the Morris Canal went on the drawing boards. A survey of the terrain between New York Harbor and the Lehigh River of Pennsylvania, a 55-mile distance as the crow flies, showed that the proposed canal route would be 102 miles. The route would proceed from New York Harbor, through the Kill Van Kull into Newark Bay, then up the Passaic River to Little Falls. A canal would then be dug to the south end of Lake Hopatcong, and from there it would lead southwest to the Delaware River, just opposite the Lehigh River and south of Easton, Pennsylvania, and Phillipsburg, New Jersey. Since the Delaware River is not navigable to either the north or south at this point, the Morris Canal would only be useful as a connection to the Lehigh Valley coal mines. The proposed route meant raising the barges 914 feet over the mountains, which was to be done on dry land and not through the use of locks. To accomplish the task, twenty-three inclined planes with tracks would be needed. In the spring of 1832, the Morris Canal

Chart 1.3 Kill Van Kull, Newark Bay, and northern Arthur Kill (reproduced from NOAA's Chart #12327)

opened. Years later the eastern end of the canal was extended through Bayonne and Jersey City, providing an even more direct route to New York Harbor.

The allure of canals was brief, however, and the four-mile-an-hour canal traffic finally succumbed to the steam locomotive. After 1860 the Morris Canal started into a decline that finally ended in 1924 when it was abandoned.

The Hackensack River, which branches off Newark Bay to the northeast, is navigable by boat as far as the town of Hackensack, although also crossed by a variety of fixed bridges and drawbridges. The Hackensack River begins in the hills of New York State, and in its lower reaches the banks of the river are a mixture of wetlands and industry. Unfortunately, water quality in the Hackensack is poor, containing metals, PCBs, dioxins, bacteria, and petroleum. Paradoxically, as with Newark Bay, the Hackensack abounds with marine life. It is common to see the banks of the Hackensack crowded with fishers and crabbers, although the fishing advisory says there should be no taking of crabs or of stripers.

Skippers with large boats who would like to take a trip up the Hackensack and anticipate opening bridges along the way may well want to reconsider. Most of the bridges have restricted opening hours. Some bridges require a one-hour notice and others require as much as an eight-hour notice. The river also has a great deal of commercial traffic, as barges and tugboats ply the waters all the way to the head of navigation at Hackensack, where there is an oil terminal.

During the 1600s the waterways of this area were the realm of pirates who preyed on the commerce of Hoboken, Jersey City, and New York City both by land and by sea. In 1695 the governor of New York, Edward Fletcher, who was perfectly willing to take bribes from the pirates and look the other way, was replaced by the Earl of Bellomont, who arrived from England with orders to clean up the cutthroats. The pirates retreated up the Hackensack River and continued their rampages. Finally, in 1797, the citizens had had enough and formed a vigilante group, with volunteers from Bergen County and from New York City, determined to eliminate the pirates once and for all. Outnumbered, the pirates disappeared into the undergrowth of the meadowlands. This area was set afire. The south wind fanned the flames and drove the pirates up to Rutherford, into the arms of vigilantes, ending the one-hundred-year reign of the Hackensack pirates.

As we continue our cruise through these waters, once the realm of pirates, we see on the chart that an alternative route to Raritan Bay is available. It is a protected and interesting alternate route, completely different from the trip through The Narrows.

At the juncture of the Kill Van Kull, Arthur Kill, and the channel into Newark Bay, be sure not to short-cut the channels between Newark Bay and the Arthur

Kill just north of Shooters Island, where there is a submerged dike and very shallow water. In recent years Shooters Island, to the south, has developed into a wildlife sanctuary.

Along the Arthur Kill derelict barges and old ships are in the tidal flats off-channel, so search the surface of the water carefully for debris. Each year more of these derelicts are being removed, but it's a slow process.

Traveling down the Arthur Kill (*Kill* is a Dutch word that means channel, stream, creek, or river) the shoreline is a maze of refineries, storage tanks, rail-road tracks, and docks and carries an unmistakable odor of petrochemicals, the same smell that permeates this area along the New Jersey Turnpike, only a half-mile to our west. But how can we complain, when the very boat we're traveling in makes use of these products, both as a means of propulsion and as the principle component in the manufacture of the fiberglass hull.

The first bridge we encounter is a railroad lift bridge that is no longer in service and is permanently in the lifted position. Although the bridge has been unused for years, there has been talk of reactivating the span. Three hundred yards to the south of the railroad bridge is the Goethals Bridge, a high, arching, cantilevered structure. The bridge was named for George Washington Goethal, the chief consulting engineer for the Port Authority of New York and New Jersey, who gained fame when he completed the Panama Canal after the French abandoned the project.

As we proceed down the Arthur Kill, we need to be aware of a buoy reversal. When we entered the Kill Van Kull from New York Harbor, we were going inland and buoys were *red, right, returning,* as would be expected. But as we proceed down the Arthur Kill, we are now heading out to sea again, and although proper, this sudden buoy reversal can be a source of confusion. Double-check the charts.

Just before the Rahway River branches off to the west we pass Pralls Island, a bird sanctuary. Although in an unlikely location, it sports an ever-increasing population of gulls and herons, who share the shoreline with factories and oil refineries. Pralls Island is one of three islands on the Arthur Kill that supports the return of ospreys to the area. In fact the whole Raritan Bay region is seeing an increase in nesting ospreys each year—a litmus test to an improving environment.

The Rahway River, which branches off into the New Jersey suburbs, is navigable well inland and is noted for spectacular fishing. Because of an accumulation of bottom sediments such as metals, PCBs, dioxins, and other toxins, fish taken here should be eaten sparingly and with the fatty tissues removed, or not at all. Unfortunately there are many people in the metropolitan area who fish for sustenance, and fish taken from contaminated streams such as this present a potential source of health problems.

Shoal-draft craft can navigate the river up to the Rahway Yacht Club, a club near the head of navigation that has the ambience of the clubs of yesteryear.

At the juncture of the Rahway River and Arthur Kill there is a plan underway to purchase about six hundred acres of land, with Green Acres and oil-spill money, to be used as a wildlife preserve.

Below the Rahway River, the Fresh Kills goes east into Staten Island, where a huge garbage landfill is creating a mountain that approaches five hundred feet in height.

About a mile below the Fresh Kills, Arthur Kill takes a sharp turn to the west (chart 1.4). On the Staten Island side of this bend is a ships' graveyard, and just beyond the bend is an electric generating plant on the New Jersey shore. South of this point the waterway takes on a less industrial and more residential and recreational atmosphere.

New Jersey's navigable waters reveal great contrasts, and none more so than the entrance to the picturesque little stream of Smith Creek, which branches off the Arthur Kill amidst oil tanks, large ships, and a PSE&G generating plant. Smith Creek, on the New Jersey shore, has a marked entrance and is easily navigable. Up the stream are marinas serving small craft, which offer slips for transients, fuel, ice, package goods, repairs, and winter storage. On the west side of the creek there are boat slips all along the shore, while on the east there are woods and marshlands. The ambience is more reminiscent of a stream on the eastern shore of the Chesapeake than of a waterway in the most densely populated area in the United States. Even if no services or supplies are required, a side trip a little way up the creek is enough to elicit exclamations from all aboard.

Farther south on the Arthur Kill there is another high cantilevered bridge, the Outerbridge Crossing, a major highway artery between New Jersey and Staten Island, and eventually one comes to the Verrazano Bridge. Most people assume that the Outerbridge Crossing was named because it is the most outer, or seaward, of the bridges connecting New Jersey and Staten Island. This is only partially true. At the time the bridge was being constructed the Port Authority of New York and New Jersey was just being organized, and the "father of the Port Authority" was an administrator named Eugenius Harvey Outerbridge. In 1926, when the new bridge across the Arthur Kill was opened, employees at the Port Authority, in the spirit of a pun, named the new bridge the Outerbridge Crossing.

Just below the Outerbridge Crossing, on the Staten Island shore, there are

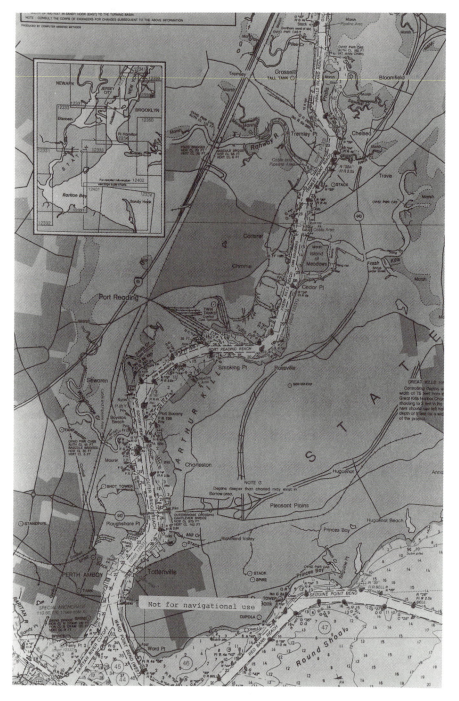

Chart 1.4 Southern Arthur Kill (reproduced from NOAA's Chart #12327)

The entrance to Smiths Creek, off Arthur Kill

Smiths Creek, off Arthur Kill

Looking north at the Outerbridge Crossing, on southern Arthur Kill

The Staten Island train terminal and remains of the old ferry slip south of the Outerbridge Crossing.

The Perth Amboy Yacht Club on the Arthur Kill near Raritan Bay

Launching ramp and park on the Arthur Kill in Perth Amboy

Staten Island homes on the shore of the lower Arthur Kill

The Perth Amboy shoreline bordering the Arthur Kill

marinas offering small-craft services, including repairs. Just beyond the marinas there is a train yard that can be seen from the water, with the remains of an old ferry pier next to it. In years past, people from Manhattan could take the ferry to Staten Island, the train to this point, another ferry across the Arthur Kill, and finally a train to the New Jersey shore or to destinations farther west.

As we head south on the Arthur Kill, we see large expensive residential homes that dot the shoreline on Staten Island. South of the Outerbridge Crossing on the New Jersey shore, as we approach Raritan Bay, is the Armory Restaurant, a brick building near the new Municipal Marina. Just beyond that we pass the Perth Amboy Yacht Club, where sailboat races are held on summer weekends. The yacht club has guest moorings and reciprocal privileges. Just south of the yacht club, on the southeastern tip of Perth Amboy, where Arthur Kill joins Raritan Bay, there is an attractive new town park along the waterfront.

While taking my first trip through the kills around Staten Island, I found it so interesting that I kept wondering why I had never done it before. Although not on the itinerary of most cruising boaters, this exploration is well worth taking at least once. It provides a whole new insight into the industrial waterways of New Jersey that lie in the shadow of the Big Apple. The trip is a panorama of contrasts and definitely not what your preconceived notions would lead you to expect.

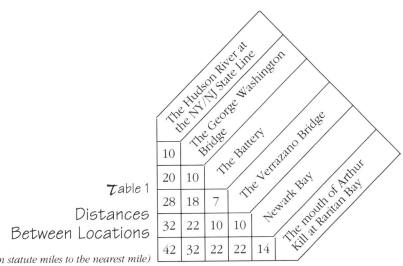

Table 1

Distances Between Locations

(in statute miles to the nearest mile)

	The Hudson River at the NY/NJ State Line	The George Washington Bridge	The Battery	The Verrazzano Bridge	Newark Bay	The mouth of Arthur Kill at Raritan Bay
	10					
	20	10				
	28	18	7			
	32	22	10	10		
	42	32	22	22	14	

Chapter Two

The Lower Bay, Sandy Hook Bay, Raritan Bay, and Their Tributaries

*F*or most cruising skippers, Sandy Hook Bay and Raritan Bay are merely stopover points on a trip north or south. It's a place to wait out the weather in a protected overnight anchorage or at a slip in a marina; usually the primary concern is to select a spot from which to continue on the next day as rapidly as possible. Those who rush on are missing a fascinating cruising locale right at their doorstep—Sandy Hook Bay, Raritan Bay, and their tributaries.

Passing south through The Narrows, which is spanned by the Verrazano Bridge, we find ourselves in New York's Lower Bay. On a clear day we can see Sandy Hook and the Atlantic Highlands of New Jersey in the distance. The north tip of the hook is only 9 miles away, and the highlands is 5 miles further south.

In the 1930s a project to build a bridge across The Narrows was on the verge of fruition, but with the likelihood of war in Europe, it was shelved. The fear was that a bridge across The Narrows could be the target of shelling or sabotage, and if it collapsed into the water, it could effectively close off the Port of New York, a port vital to any war effort.

When war did come to our shores German U-boats operated virtually unimpeded along the Atlantic Coast of North America (in Germany's Operation Paukenschlag), under the command of Admiral Karl Donitz. During that brief period more than 400 Allied ships were sent to the bottom of the ocean between Canada and Panama—a greater catastrophe in the loss of lives and of ship tonnage than was the attack on Pearl Harbor. Virtually no counter-measures were taken. In fact, coastal hotel and amusement-park lights were left on so the tourist business would not suffer; the lights created perfect silhouettes of the cargo ships and tankers and were an immense aid to German U-boats activity. Even lighthouses, navigation buoys, and ships displayed their normal lights.

There was also the very real possibility that U-boats would enter New York Harbor through The Narrows to destroy the convoys anchored there. To counter this, a submarine net was set up along the shore just south of where the Verrazano Bridge now stands. The net could be stretched across The Narrows to deter the German U-boats and thus protect the troopships, tankers, and cargo ships inside New York Harbor.

My most memorable trip through The Narrows, in the days before the Verrazano Bridge existed, took place on a troopship returning from Europe after World War II. As we entered New York Harbor, we saw, to our right, a huge sign that was laid out on the grassy slopes of Brooklyn Heights; it said: "Welcome Home." To our left stood the Statue of Liberty, with her arm raised in salutation. Every GI on board had tears in his eyes—we were finally home. Coincidently, my father had made that same entrance into New York Harbor a quarter of a century earlier when returning from France after World War I. I'm thankful that our son, Tom, was not obliged to repeat the tradition.

From The Narrows, on a clear day, we can see New Jersey's Atlantic Highlands and Sandy Hook, forming the southeast boundary of Sandy Hook Bay. The trip from The Narrows to Sandy Hook poses no special problems when there is adequate visibility and when sea conditions are satisfactory. We need to be aware, however, that the buoyed channels crisscrossing the bay are used by major shipping. Depths required by recreational boats are good almost everywhere, so traveling outside the marked channels is not only acceptable, but it keeps us out of the heavy commercial traffic. Crossing the bay on a foggy day is quite another story. Once, my wife, Elsie, and I, under pressure of schedule, decided to cross in a heavy fog. Traveling with Loran but no radar, we had only gone a few hundred yards when we heard the rumble of massive engines approaching, and a tug pushing a barge emerged from the mist on a parallel course, about fifty feet away. We decided to turn back and wait until the fog cleared. Those using radar, and confident of their skills, may elect to do otherwise.

When strong and prolonged winds are blowing from the east or southeast, the trip between The Narrows and Sandy Hook can be very rough, and even dangerous, for a small open boat. Under these circumstances there is always the option of using the kills around the west side of Staten Island (the alternate route that was described in chapter 1).

These waters south of New York City are where New York and New Jersey's largest rivers meet the Atlantic Ocean. This harbor estuary is an oasis of life that has suffered greatly from urbanization and industrialization. In 1990 the

American Littoral Society established the "Baykeeper" program to provide a unified voice in the advocacy of marine and shore protection and to seek solutions to environmental problems in the estuary.

Andrew Willner, the baykeeper for the New Jersey/New York Harbor, patrols the waters in a boat powered by a diesel engine that can run on soy-bean oil. He tracks down sources of litter, liquid poisons, and slicks of chemicals or oils that escape from ships or from unseen pipes. He is the spokesperson and conscience of the harbor estuary who, along with a network of volunteers from all walks of life, monitors water quality parameters every two weeks at strategic locations and watches for polluters of these beleaguered waters. The baykeepers are the vanguard in the peaceful citizens' battle against water pollution, and they deserve the thanks of all who have concern for our environment. They offer a tangible ray of hope for reversing more than two hundred years worth of damage to our fragile marine ecosystem.

Surprisingly, the major source of pollution to these waters now is not from "point-source" pollution, that is, from industries or sewage disposal. Instead, the major culprit is "nonpoint-source" or pollution from lawn chemicals, farms, road runoff, and the like. Cindy Zipf, executive director of *Clean Ocean Action*, aptly described it as "pointless pollution."

New restrictions on ocean dumping have gone a long way toward ameliorating the problem, and New York's sewage sludge, which was once dumped offshore, is now shipped by railroad tank cars to farms in Texas for use as fertilizer.

One of the parameters used to indicate healthy water quality, or water that will support marine life, is dissolved oxygen. In the 1950s and 1960s a simple test for dissolved oxygen entailed taking a healthy fish and putting it in the bay's waters, and timing how many seconds it would take the fish to die. Now, with the greatly improved water quality, marine life and a variety of species are returning to the estuary in ever increasing numbers, and dissolved oxygen is at levels compatible with healthy marine procreation.

As we continue on, we head toward the destination for most transients, the marinas on the south, under the hills of the highlands, or an anchorage such as Horseshoe Cove, inside of Sandy Hook. From the Verrazano Bridge, it's a straight-line trip across the bay to these locations. As we head south from The Narrows, we pass the tiny Hoffman and Swinburne islands to the west of the marked channel. The New Jersey/New York state line runs roughly east and west down the center of the bay, midway between the New Jersey Highlands and The Narrows, so those who have traveled to the east of Staten Island are now returning to New Jersey waters.

The 80-square-mile bay supports an amazing variety of fish, shellfish, and

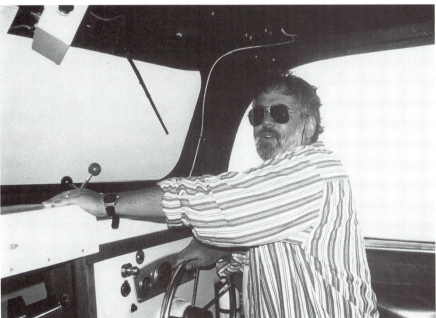

The New Jersey/New York Baykeeper, on Raritan Bay (top photo courtesy of Bill Schultz, Baykeeper Auxilliary)

crustaceans; in fact, lobster traps are now being used in the bay and are yielding a reasonable catch. The bottom of the bay is covered with clams, more than in any other region of New Jersey, but they are off-limits for recreational harvesting. A few years ago a program was set up so that commercially harvested bay clams, under strict supervision by the state, could be transported to Lacey Township in Ocean County, where a "clam relay station" has been set up in Barnegat Bay. The clams are left in the clean waters of the bay for up to sixty days, depending on the time of year. There they purge themselves of any toxins and can then be sold commercially.

In 1991 the Port Authority awarded Atlantic Highlands a $1.3 million grant to build a clam depuration plant—a plant that uses oxygen, cold, pure water, and ultraviolet light to kill harmful bacteria. This will be more convenient than transporting the clams to Barnegat Bay or to the only other depuration plant, located in Sea Bright.

During World War I and World War II, Sandy Hook served as an artillery base, ostensibly used as an area from which to guard the entrance to New York Harbor. Sandy Hook's armament included Nike missiles before its military career came to an end in 1975. At its northern tip, the old ammunition bunkers and gun emplacements of Fort Hancock and the historic Sandy Hook Light-

The Sandy Hook Lighthouse as seen from Sandy Hook Bay

house share space with a Coast Guard base. The majority of the land on Sandy Hook is now under the jurisdiction of the National Park Service.

The popular anchorage of Horseshoe Cove is about two miles down from the tip of Sandy Hook on the bay side. The approach to Horseshoe Cove from the north takes us past yellow-brick buildings that were once used as officers' quarters. Just beyond is the rubble of concrete bunkers at water's edge, remnants of World War II. These bunkers are just to the north of Horseshoe Cove and serve as a good landmark. Fish nets extend into the bay, well out from shore. Make the approach outside of these nets. There is a sandspit extending south that encloses the northwest side of the cove and stretches under water for a considerable distance. Portions of it are awash at low tide. The southern end of this underwater bar is marked by a white can buoy with a red diamond. Entering the cove south of this buoy is the rule. The other similar white buoys at the south end of the anchorage are no-wake markers. On shore, near the footbridge at the north end of the anchorage, are drums for garbage and recyclables. Horseshoe Cove is a popular anchorage, and on summer weekends can be crowded. It's a good idea to check the weather report before anchoring; the cove offers no protection from west winds, which can make for an uncomfortable overnight stay.

The World War II bunker ruins just north of Horseshoe Cove

Along the south shore of Sandy Hook Bay are several marinas, of which the Atlantic Highlands Municipal Marina is the largest. Transients who would like to anchor at the Municipal Marina for the night can drop the hook within the long stone breakwater if there is room, (stay out of the approach channel to the marina) or they can take a slip in the 500-boat marina that's capable of accommodating the largest of craft. The docks here are not floating, and because of the high tidal range, the vertical ladders inside the slips are an awkward means of going ashore. Care must also be taken when setting up dock lines. If too tight, they'll limit the boat's rise and fall with the tide. If too loose, there's the risk of banging into the barnacle-encrusted pilings. This is a full-service marina, which includes a restaurant, showers, tennis courts, and other amenities within walking distance. Although not shown on the charts, there seems to be a magnetic anomaly in this area, so be wary.

The hill of the Highlands has been important to navigation since the first explorers used it as the landmark to locate the entrance to New York Harbor. Frequently the old sailing ships would stop at the foot of the highlands, in Sandy Hook Bay, to replenish their water supply from the "spout," a clear, cool spring that still flows today. The 1609 log from Henry Hudson's *Half Moon* shows that he dropped anchor there and sent his men ashore for water. Captain Kidd put into New Jersey often—to bury treasure, say the romantics. More probably his

Henry Hudson's spring

stops at the Highlands were to fill his water casks before a privateering foray. The spring was first used by the Lenape Indians (whose name appropriately means "first people"), and then by the early European settlers, but the spring's water flow has diminished greatly since those days. It is now locally known as "Henry Hudson's Spring," and a bronze plaque nearby commemorates its history.

After a quiet night at an anchorage or in a marina, it's now time to explore Sandy Hook Bay, Raritan Bay, and their tributaries. Sandy Hook, on the east, is part of the National Gateway Recreation Area, with facilities including ocean and bay swimming beaches, surf fishing, nature trails, and picnic areas. At the Spermaceti Cove Visitor's Center near the entrance to the Recreation Area are maps and brochures. The Sandy Hook Lighthouse, an eighty-eight foot octagonal tower, the oldest working lighthouse in the country, is now a historical monument. In 1762, when Sandy Hook's lighthouse was built, it was just 500 feet from the tip of the hook, the logical location from which to guide boats through the deep-water channel that leads into Sandy Hook Bay. Since then Sandy Hook has been extending north, so much so that the lighthouse now stands more than a mile and a half from the hook's northern tip. Such is our ever-changing coastline.

At the southeastern corner of Sandy Hook Bay is a waterway that leads to the "twin rivers," the Navesink and the Shrewsbury (chart 2.1). This area was the setting for James Fenimore Cooper's novel *The Water-Witch*, the name of a ghost ship that sailed Sandy Hook Bay's waters in the early 1700s. The entrance to the Shrewsbury River is via a buoyed channel that passes through the bascule bridge (with a 35-foot closed clearance) that connects the Highlands with the ocean beaches. Tides in this waterway can be swift, and auxiliaries should allow for a delayed bridge opening and congested boat traffic. When awaiting the opening of the bridge, be aware that just before the bridge on the bay side and off the main channel, are the piers of an old railroad bridge, some of which are submerged or awash at high tide. Adjacent to the bascule bridge is Bahr's Restaurant and Marina, one of the oldest on the New Jersey shore.

Just past the bridge, the Navesink River, which is more of a tidal estuary than a true river, branches off to the west, and has a navigable channel for 6 miles up to Red Bank. In Red Bank only small craft will be able to go farther up river, beyond the fixed Route 35 highway bridge (with an 8-foot clearance) near the head of navigation. The Navesink was originally called the North Shrewsbury, confirming their relationship as twins. The channel entering the Navesink cuts between shoals, and the channel depth at low tide has been reported to be 2.5 feet in spots, so straying outside the marked channel can easily create a delay until the next tide change. Once past the bascule bridge (with a 22-foot

The waterway and bascule bridge to the Navesink and Shrewsbury rivers

closed clearance) and the shoals, facilities for transients are on the south shore, and anchorages with good holding can be found under the high bluffs in this residential environment, which is one of the most beautiful estuaries along our coastline. At the head of navigation, about five and a half miles up from the entrance, is the town of Red Bank, where docking facilities, shops, transportation to New York City, restaurants at water's edge, and the Riverview Medical Center are located.

Perhaps the most famous of the restaurants along the banks of the Navesink in Red Bank is the Molly Pitcher Inn and Marina, located on the south bank near the Route 35 bridge. The inn, a landmark since 1928, is easily recognizable, designed to resemble Philadelphia's Independence Hall. It is named, of course, for the heroine of the battle of Monmouth during the Revolution. The 70-slip marina at the foot of the hill below the inn has sixteen docks for transients, can accommodate large vessels, and is a short walk from the stores in town. On weekends there is a two-night-minimum stay at the marina.

The waters of the Navesink have been steadily improving during the last few years. This is due to a joint program that was implemented by federal, state, and local agencies. The water quality is so good that, for the first time in nearly thirty years, the Department of Environmental Protection has recommended the

Chart 2.1 Navesink and Shrewsbury rivers (reproduced from NOAA's Chart #12324)

The Navesink River

opening of 1,070 acres of river bottom (east of McClees Creek) for the direct harvest of soft clams during the winter season.

If one follows the waterway from Sandy Hook Bay, and past the entrance to the Navesink, and under the bridge that joins Rumson Neck and Sea Bright (with a 15-foot closed clearance), one will enter into the bay portion of the Shrewsbury River. The bascule bridge across the entrance to this section of the Shrewsbury has restricted hours on summer weekends and holidays; they are 9 A.M. to 7 P.M. Openings are on the hour and the half-hour. During these times, especially on weekends, the narrow channel width and the congested boat traffic can make the passage hectic for those awaiting an opening.

This part of the Shrewsbury is one of the prettiest of any of New Jersey's inland tidewaters and always reminds me of a miniature Chesapeake Bay. Not only is the similarity of the natural features striking (if one looks at the chart), but the ambience is the same. The banks of the bay are serrated with coves, brooks, streams, and miniestuaries, and along the banks are private docks, yacht clubs, marinas, and shoreside restaurants, along with homes that range in size from mansions to condominiums. Most of the Shrewsbury is shallow, but the channels off the main waterway are well marked, and an exploration of the many little side streams and coves by dinghy can provide an enchanting sojourn.

The Shrewsbury River

As we cruise through these waters, many maritime anecdotes from the past come to mind. It was just a century ago, in 1894, that Simon Lake, a native of Toms River, made one of the world's first submarines. The *Argonaut Junior* was fourteen feet long, made of yellow pine, and designed so that when submerged it could travel along the bottom of the river or bay on its three wheels, powered by a hand crank. A compressed-air soda-fountain tank provided the pressurization. The submarine was launched at Atlantic Highlands, and Simon Lake Drive now marks the launching spot. From there it was paddled to the Shrewsbury River, where the crew made their first underwater run, traveling along the bottom of the Shrewsbury at a moderate walking gait.

Lake's later designs were sold to the U.S. Navy, as well as to several European nations, and included his inventions of the periscope and torpedo tubes. These contracts grossed millions, but Lake was a poor businessman and died in poverty in 1945.

We now leave these historic river estuaries and head back to Sandy Hook Bay, where we continue our exploration of the shoreline, heading west from the hook toward the separately named but indistinguishable waters of Raritan Bay.

In the spring of 1994, New Jersey announced that the 181-slip Leonardo State Marina, located in Middletown Township, on the south shore of Sandy

Hook Bay, would be put up for sale. Since then, the proposal has been withdrawn. (The Leonardo Marina is one of four owned by the state. The others are the 125-slip Forked River Marina in Lacey Township, off Barnegat Bay; the 685-slip Senator Frank S. Farley State Marina in Atlantic City; and the 115-slip Fortescue State Marina in Cumberland County on the north shore of Delaware Bay).

Note that a security zone exists around the two-mile-long government pier that extends out into the bay just west of the Leonardo State Marina—stay well away. This pier is used for loading and unloading munitions, as would be indicated by its name, the Earle Ammunition Pier. In May of 1950 an ammunition explosion occurred on the docks, killing thirty-one dock workers, shattering doors and windows for miles around, and showering debris and soot over a huge area. The explosion was heard as far away as Pennsylvania.

To the west of the Earle Ammunition Pier, pound nets can be encountered along shore, making nighttime travel difficult, or even hazardous. We've seen these nets off Port Monmouth, Keansburg, and along shore to the east of Cheesequake Creek. Although required to be lighted, the dim lights are often difficult to separate from the lights on shore. Occasionally small strobe lights mark the nets, and some have radar reflectors on the poles.

All along the southern shoreline of Raritan Bay there are municipal and

The government pier in Sandy Hook Bay

The fishing fleet in Belford Harbor

county beaches. Water quality is checked regularly, and in recent years there have been few closings.

Compton Creek and Belford Harbor, just west of the government pier, are devoted to commercial fishing boats, seiners, draggers, lobsterers, and the like. In Belford Harbor the fishing captains established the Belford Seafood Cooperative in 1956, which is housed in a large building beside the water. Fish are sold both wholesale and retail. The harbor is reminiscent of a New England fishing village, but a conflict looms between the commercial fishers and the proposed waterfront developers who would displace their lifestyle. The proposed development, which would be along the shore to the west of the creek, would include 5,000 residential units, shopping centers, office buildings, and a new breakwater enclosing a 700-boat marina. There is also a proposal for a ferry service to Manhattan from Belford Harbor, which would require widening the waterway, dredging, and constructing bulkheads. All of the proposed projects are of concern to environmentalists as well as to commercial fishers. Currently it is unlikely that a recreational boat would find a berth in Belford Harbor, but a cruise through the harbor is a fascinating diversion, as the traveler briefly visits the world of the commercial ocean fisher. To enter, follow the entrance buoys in off the bay. At the last buoy, just before shore, a ninety degree left turn takes one south of the high stone breakwater and into the harbor.

During our last entrance into Belford Harbor, one hundred large concrete castings were lined up on shore near the entrance breakwater. These were the final sections of the patented "beachsaver" reefs that were to be put into the ocean off Belmar and Spring Lake.

The beachsaver reefs have since been put in place as a way of saving and stabilizing the beaches in lieu of old tires, ships, and Vietnam War tanks (the latter recently placed offshore to provide a home for sea life).

According to the U.S. Geological Survey, half of all beach-replenishment sand is gone within two years, and the state's $2 million Pilot Reef Project will determine whether the twenty-one-ton interlocking beachsaver modules can halt or slow the process. (Cranes lower the units to the ocean floor about three hundred feet off the beach, and divers position them in place.) At Belmar and Spring Lake this artificial reef stretches for about one thousand feet, with the top of the units three to seven feet below the surface at low tide. The first reef was installed off Avalon, the second off Cape May Point, and the reef off Belmar was the third in the series. By the end of 1994, the results at Belmar, Spring Lake, and Cape May looked promising, while the Avalon reef had produced mixed results—but it is still too early to predict the long-term effects.

About a mile northwest of Compton Creek is Pews Creek, where about six

The beachsaver, artificial reefs onshore at Belford Harbor, awaiting placement in the ocean off Belmar and Spring Lake

feet of water exists to the marinas. Inside the creek, on its east shore, is a new large marina and park operated by the Monmouth County Park Commission, and just beyond is a private marina. Sailors should note that the private marina does not accept transient sailboats. The chart shows a bridge across the creek near the entrance that hasn't existed since 1970. Thorns Creek at Keansburg also has some limited facilities for small-to-medium sized craft.

Matawan Creek at Keyport is easily entered through its buoyed entrance channel. The Keyport Yacht Club and a marina are just to the east of the entrance to the creek, and the entrance channel continues past moored sailboats on both east and west sides. These moored boats, easily seen with the aid of field glasses from the bay, provide a good landmark for Matawan Creek's entrance channel. Once inside, the fishing fleet is immediately to port, followed by the town dock, which is suitable for use by ship's tender. There are marinas on both sides of the channel before the first bridge (that has a 6-foot clearance) as well as farther up the waterway, beyond this bridge and the following 12-foot fixed bridge. Stores, restaurants, and a Ferry Museum are within walking distance of the marinas.

Farther west along the south shore of Raritan Bay is Cheesequake Creek. The entrance is between stone breakwaters with skeletal towers on their outer

The distinctive headlands at Keyport can be easily identified through the haze

The entrance to Cheesequake Creek off Raritan Bay

ends. The easterly breakwater is submerged at high tide and will not show up on radar, so a short cut will put you on the rocks. On weekends there are many boats anchored off the beaches in this area, where the hard sand bottom provides good holding. The Route 35 bascule bridge (with closed clearance of 25 feet) is just inside the entrance to the creek. There are marinas on Stumps Creek, which branches off Cheesequake Creek to the east, beyond the bascule bridge but ahead of the railroad bridge. The railroad bridge (with closed clearance of 3 feet) is usually in the open position, unless a train is expected. Locally, the Cheesequake is called Morgan's Creek so, when calling the railroad bridge tender, call for Morgan railroad bridge. Further up Cheesequake Creek, beyond the railroad bridge, there are several large marinas that one passes before reaching the Garden State Parkway's 8-foot fixed bridges. These marinas are very popular with recreational boaters, particularly those who own sailboats, in spite of some typical bridge-opening problems. The Cheesequake was once the home of the famous Luhr Boatyard, where Henry Luhr's beautiful wooden boats were built for many years, prior to the popularity of fiberglass.

Two and a half miles due north from Cheesequake Creek, across this western corner of Raritan Bay, is the entrance to the Arthur Kill, which separates New Jersey and Staten Island. (Arthur Kill was described in chapter 1.) At one

Cheesequake Creek, with the Garden State Parkway Bridge in the background

time this western end of Raritan Bay contained one of the best oyster grounds on the east coast, until pollution and sediment accumulation destroyed it.

To the west is the entrance to the Raritan River, with South Amboy on its south bank and Perth Amboy on its north bank (chart 2.2). The name "Amboy" derives from the original 1651 land deed (the land was deeded from the Lenape Indians), when the area was called "Empoyle." This became "Ampoyle," then "Ambo," and finally "Amboy."

The Raritan River flows eleven miles through meadowlands that have been virtually untouched by industry or development, finally reaching the head of navigation at New Brunswick, the home of Rutgers University.

The Raritan is the longest river within New Jersey, approximately one hundred miles in length from the headwaters of the south branch to Raritan Bay. The name Raritan can be traced to the Naraticong Indian tribe of the Raritang nation, who lived along the river and used the river as their primary mode of travel.

Long before the most primitive of roads had been established, the Native Americans had beaten a trail across the state that was later used to carry furs for trade in the New York City area. The trail was forged from the most southerly of

The entrance to Arthur Kill as seen from Raritan Bay

The entrance to the Raritan River as seen from Raritan Bay

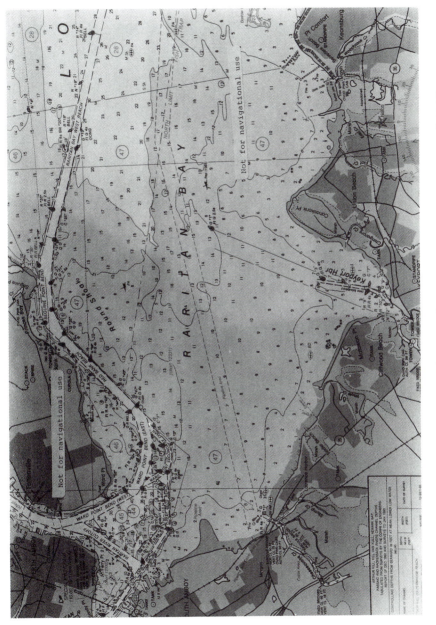

Chart 2.2 Western end of Raritan Bay (reproduced from NOAA's Chart #12327)

the Delaware River's fording areas, the rapids at Trenton, to the most easterly of the fording areas on the Raritan, near the present city of New Brunswick, and then on to New York. Old deeds referred to it as the Indian Path, and it finally became the dividing line between Somerset and Middlesex counties.

In later years the trail became an important stagecoach thoroughfare; then a railroad right-of-way; and finally an automobile artery, the New Jersey Turnpike, one of the busiest highways in the world.

During the early years of colonization, captains brought their sailing ships up the Raritan River to fill their water casks before long voyages because the water was so sweet and pure. Eventually, an increase in population and a gross disregard for the basic tenets of ecology and sanitation created impurities in the Raritan's waters, making it unusable for fish, fowl, and humans. It wasn't until the mid-1920s that the government started to acknowledge the problem, and only in recent years, under pressure from environmental groups, have concrete steps been taken and the quality of the river's water improved.

At the entrance to the Raritan River is a railroad swing bridge, which is normally open, except when commuter trains are approaching. This is followed by a highway swing bridge, the Victory Highway Bridge (with a 28-foot closed clearance), where only the northern span should be used. The high twin fixed bridges of Route 9 and the Garden State Parkway come next. Just beyond the Parkway bridge, on the south shore, there was, at one time, a lead and titanium pigment plant and its disposal pond, which is easily seen by motorists crossing the Garden State Parkway Bridge over the Raritan River. It is, thankfully, no longer in operation.

Beyond the Parkway bridge, there are no additional bridges for 7 miles, and then one reaches the 45-foot fixed bridge of the New Jersey Turnpike, just before entering New Brunswick and Highland Park. Since there is virtually no industry along this segment of the river, commercial traffic is almost nonexistent, and the trip is a pleasant winding tour through marshlands.

About five miles west of the Parkway bridge, the tributary of Washington Canal branches off to the south and is navigable for several miles.

Farther up the Raritan, just west of the New Jersey Turnpike Bridge, one approaches New Brunswick on the south bank and Highland Park on the north bank. This is where the river ceases to be navigable, but it wasn't always so. At one time, it was the starting point of the Delaware and Raritan Canal, an important commercial link between the port of New York and the Delaware River near Trenton and Philadelphia.

The idea of a canal connecting the Raritan and Delaware rivers across the narrow, 35-mile wide, waist of New Jersey had been discussed since earliest colonial times. The advantages were obvious. The industrial ports of New York City and of northern New Jersey could be connected with those of Philadelphia, Camden, and Trenton, eliminating the torturous trip of more than 260 miles out into the Atlantic, through Delaware Bay, and up the Delaware River. Since the Raritan River flowed due west at this point, it was a natural location for the connecting link. Digging was finally begun in 1804 and completed in 1829. Although, as the crow flies, it is only about twenty-five miles from New Brunswick to the Delaware River, due to the topography the canal trip was 44 miles long, ending in Bordentown, just south of Trenton.

As soon as the canal opened the traffic was heavy, rivaling the tonnage and revenue of the Erie Canal, but the canals in the northeast were already being threatened by the railroads. In the same decade that the Delaware and Raritan Canal began hauling freight and passengers, the railroads increased their miles of track from a mere 23 miles in 1830 to more than 2,800 miles by 1840. It wasn't long before railroads were moving more freight at a higher speed, and canals fell into disuse. The Delaware and Raritan Canal was finally closed, and many sections were filled in. We're fortunate that long sections of the canal have been preserved and are now a part of county and state park systems, conserving this

The Delaware and Raritan Canal Park in New Brunswick

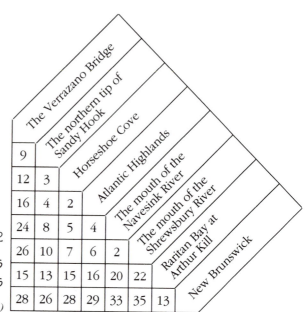

Table 2

Distances
Between Locations

(in statute miles to the nearest mile)

The Verrazano Bridge	The northern tip of Sandy Hook	Horseshoe Cove	Atlantic Highlands	The mouth of the Navesink River	The mouth of the Shrewsbury River	Raritan Bay at Arthur Kill	New Brunswick
9							
12	3						
16	4	2					
24	8	5	4				
26	10	7	6	2			
15	13	15	16	20	22		
28	26	28	29	33	35	13	

historical waterway for future generations. The parks use the canal and the original tow path along its banks for walking, biking, jogging, horseback riding, fishing, picnicking, and boating (in small boats, outboards prohibited).

*O*ur cruise throughout the Raritan Bay region now comes to a close as we prepare for the offshore passage from Sandy Hook, heading south.

Have a good night's sleep in preparation for the ocean voyage tomorrow.

 $\mathcal{C}$hapter Three

Sandy Hook to Manasquan Inlet and the Intracoastal Waterway to Toms River

$\mathcal{F}$rom our protected anchorage in Raritan Bay or in Sandy Hook Bay, we'll now take the ocean leg of our trip south. After checking the NOAA weather channel (WX-1 for New York City, WX-2 for Atlantic City) as well as checking the weather visually, and with the boat prepared for an offshore trip, we head out.

Since we do most of our cruising in our two-masted schooner *Delphinus*, we are limited to a hull speed of about seven knots maximum, so we always start our ocean trip south from the bay at first light. The typical wind pattern along the New Jersey coast and intracoastal is diurnal, that is, it has a daily recurring pattern: calm in the early morning; then, at about 11 A.M., the sea breeze begins to pick up as the land warms; wind speeds increase until about 4 P.M.; they die down again by sunset. The afternoon wind can become very strong, considerably stronger than the forecasted speed, and along with the summertime possibility of afternoon thunderstorms, this can make inlet entrances less than pleasant—so an early start in the morning is recommended.

Marginal weather should be carefully considered. When deciding whether or not to wait, take into account both the skipper's and the crew's experience and ability, as well as the seaworthiness of the boat.

The Atlantic coastline of New Jersey stretches 127 miles south from Sandy Hook. The shoreline is relatively straight, with fairly constant slope waters and a sandy bottom. Most of this coastline consists of a series of barrier islands, broken intermittently by inlets, varying from excellent to unusable. These inlets continue to form, change, or close, as storms pound vengeful waves against the barrier islands and as high seas, whipped up by nor'easters and hurricanes, recarve the coastline.

⚓ ⚓

Visual navigation along the coast in clear weather from a couple of miles offshore presents no special problems. Water towers display each town name, and the hill at the Highlands, the Ferris wheel at Seaside, Barnegat Lighthouse, the casinos and high rises at Atlantic City, and the Loran tower at Cape May, can be seen from great distances.

As we check our charts, we discover the astonishing fact that from this point, the trip by boat to Trenton, New Jersey is longer than the boat trip to Boston, Massachusetts. This is dramatic testimony to the extent of New Jersey's navigable waters.

Taking Sandy Hook Channel around the tip of Sandy Hook out into the ocean, we usually see some small local boats close to shore in False Hook Channel (chart 3.1). This is a "local knowledge" route and best left to the locals. Near the tip of the hook, a condition called the "Sandy Hook rip" exists when wind and tide are in opposition. This usually occurs just to the northwest of False Hook Channel and can make things a trifle nasty; unexpected breakers can pop up and ruin the whole day. Even though you might want to examine the fauna on Sandy Hook's nude beach, from a safety standpoint it's better to take Sandy Hook Channel out about two miles, then head south and closer to shore again, if desired. At this point, our trolling lure is lowered over the side, usually guaranteeing one or more bluefish to restock the larder before returning to inland waters.

We frequently make the trip just a few hundred yards offshore, sightseeing our way south. Once, just south of the hook, a sudden fog engulfed us and visibility decreased to just a boat-length. Advection fogs such as this are common from early spring through June and occur whenever warm, humid air overruns the, as yet, cold ocean. We had no Loran or GPS on board, but rather than return inside Sandy Hook we used our compass, depth-sounder, and an old RDF, slowly continuing our way through the sodden gray mist and following the 30-foot contour (about a mile offshore and well inside the shipping lanes) all the way down to Barnegat Inlet. We followed a relatively straight line, making for an uneventful trip, and we were happy to discover the entrance buoys to Barnegat Inlet and to return to inland waters.

South of Sandy Hook we pass the Highlands. A lighthouse has been in operation on top of the hill here since 1762. The twin towers of the present lighthouse were built in 1862 by a consortium of New York City merchants intent on averting shipwrecks; they were originally called the New York Lighthouse. (The lights were dedicated by President Lincoln.) Standing at a total height of merely 246 feet, they are, to this day, located on the highest ground on the Atlantic coast between New York and Key West. The twin lights of the

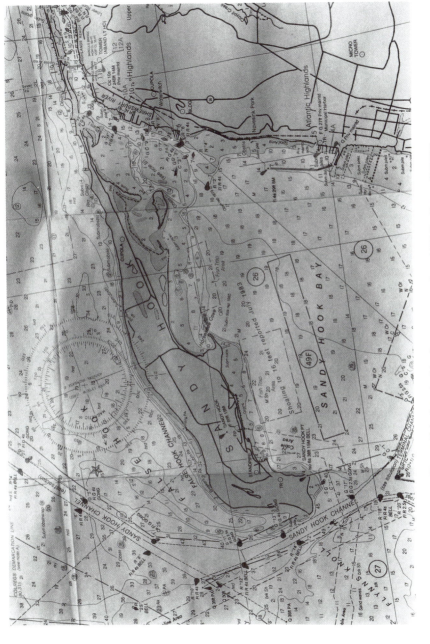

Chart 3.1 Sandy Hook (reproduced from NOAA's Chart #12327)

The ocean beach at Sandy Hook and the Sandy Hook Lighthouse

Highlands was the first view of the New World seen by tens of thousands of immigrants approaching this coastline during the evening hours.

If you look closely, you'll see that the twin towers are not identical twins. The square-shaped south tower has sixty-five steps to its top, while the octagonally-shaped north tower has sixty-four. When they were operational, the lights shone through seven-foot Fresnel lenses, providing the most powerful beacons in the country until they were decommissioned in 1949. The towers are listed on current charts as abandoned.

Traveling south from the highlands, the next major ocean-side resort is Long Branch. It was once the unofficial summer resort of U.S. presidents, and it was also the place James Garfield went to die after being mortally wounded by an assassin's bullet. The carnival games and arcades along the boardwalk were one of Long Branch's big tourist attractions until they were destroyed by fire in June 1987. From here we'll be able to see the pier at Asbury Park, jutting out into the ocean.

As one ocean-side resort follows another, we head south along the coast-line and don't even use our Loran, GPS, or radar, since checking off the route on the chart via water towers and prominent buildings is more fun. Clear, calm days, however, are the most practical time to hone navigational skills, when electronic read outs and dead reckoning can be compared to visual observa-

The Highlands and the Twin Lights

tions. Aside from the enjoyment and practice, having an up-to-date chart on board and knowing how to use it is the cheapest boat insurance on the market.

Fifteen miles south from the tip of Sandy Hook, we pass the Convention Hall Pier at Asbury Park. Each time we sail past I remember the September day in 1934 when my family gathered on the beach to see the still-burning hull of the cruise ship *Morro Castle*. It lay aground, broadside to the beach, just beyond the surf line, its stern less than one hundred yards from Asbury Park pier, and its bow close to the stone jetty. Some of the bodies of the 134 who perished had already begun to wash ashore at New Jersey's resort beaches, and it took weeks before the ship was finally towed free and eventually broken up for scrap.

In September of 1994, just over sixty years after the disaster, survivors of the *Morro Castle* disaster met at the Sea Girt Lighthouse in what may have been their last reunion. A book about the strange events that led to the ship's demise, based on recently-released government documents that were obtained through the Freedom of Information act, is now being written.

Seventeen miles below Sandy Hook and about two miles below Asbury Park is the Shark River Inlet, the only small-craft harbor between Sandy Hook and Manasquan Inlet (chart 3.2). It's a popular spot for fishing, partying, and charter-boat rides, and has small-craft facilities, but it is navigable inland less than a mile and is not connected to the New Jersey Intracoastal Waterway (the

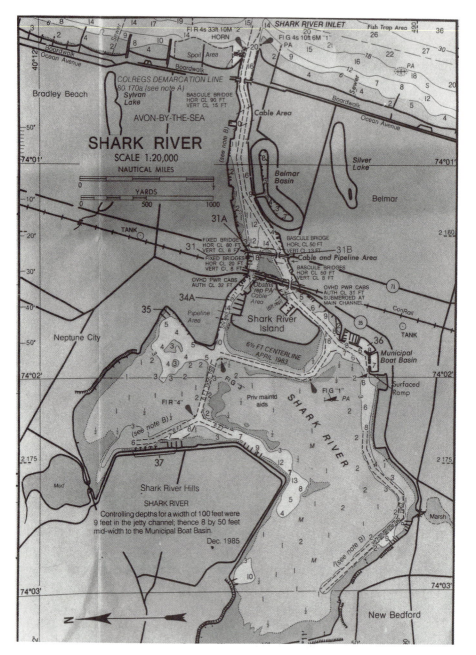

$\mathcal{C}$hart 3.2 Shark River (reproduced from NOAA's Chart #12324)

ICW) in any way. The main entrance channel is crossed by four bascule bridges, the first of which is just inside the inlet. These bridges operate as one unit and must be opened for sailboats and large powerboats. Vessels that require a bridge opening should not commit themselves to entering the inlet until the drawspan is completely open; these bridges have restricted hours during the summer months, and tidal flow in the inlet can create problems.

The Route 35 bridge across Shark River has been an irritation to boaters and motorists alike since it was opened in 1927. For years there has been talk of replacing it with a high fixed bridge, and now it looks as if it will finally happen—if federal funding is approved. The Department of Transportation plans to begin construction of a 50-foot fixed bridge in 1998, to open in the year 2000. The new bridge will actually consist of two separate spans for north and south road traffic. When the first span is completed, the old drawbridge will be demolished and work will begin on the second span.

Five miles farther south we are approaching the granite jetties at Manasquan Inlet and the beginning of the New Jersey Intracoastal Waterway. On the chart there's a "danger area" just to the north of the inlet. If large red flags are flying on shore, the area is being used as a military firing range, and staying outside the marker buoys, which are about two miles offshore, is not only prudent but required.

The outer tips of the Manasquan Inlet's breakwaters are designated as the start of New Jersey's Intracoastal Waterway, *Mile-0*, which ends at Cape May. The ICW is shown as a magenta-colored solid line on the charts, and at 5-mile intervals it is crossed by another magenta line, which indicates the number of statute miles from Mile-0. At night, when one is using a red chart light, the magenta lines look black, as intended. Frequently, in descriptions of places along this inland route, I will use these ICW mile designations as a simpler means of describing a location than latitude and longitude.

Manasquan Inlet is normally easy to use, except when tides and strong winds are in opposition. The jetties have lights on their outer ends, and the south jetty has a foghorn. The huge amount of commercial, charter, and pleasure boat traffic can make summer weekends a bit hectic. New Jersey has more than 165,000 registered boats, and sometimes it seems as if they are all trying to use Manasquan Inlet. Once inside the inlet, the towns of Brielle on the north and Point Pleasant on the south face each other across the Manasquan River. (Manasquan is a name derived from the original American Indian name "Man-atahasquawhan." "Man-a-tah" meant island; "squaw," wife; and "han," river. Translated in its entirety, it means "River Island for Wives," and it was a place Indian men left their wives when they were away hunting and fishing.)

Immediately inside the inlet at Point Pleasant on the south are the jointly

Aerial view of Manasquan Inlet (photo courtesy of Keith Hamilton, Studio-9, Waretown)

owned, adjacent restaurants The Lobster Shanty and Wharfside. To reach them, follow the marked but uncharted channel toward the fishing-fleet docks. There are slips for transients and a dinghy dock behind the breakwater and in front of the Wharfside, but an overnight stay is not permitted.

There are small-craft facilities along both shores of the Manasquan, which offer slips for transients, fuel, repairs, and haul-out services.

The largest of the Brielle marinas is the Brielle Marine Basin, just to the west of the railroad bridge. It is a family-owned business that was started more than forty years ago. Fuel, repairs, and a marine store are part of the marina, which has ten slips set aside for transients.

On the south shore of Point Pleasant, just before the Point Pleasant Canal, one will find Clarks Landing Marina. It is a sports and fishing center that caters to family-oriented activities. The marina has a restaurant and lounge and a ship's store, and boat shows are frequently hosted there. There are many more marinas and yacht clubs along this busy two-mile stretch of waterway.

As we travel west up the Manasquan River, we go through a railroad bridge that is normally open; it is very narrow, only 48 feet. This is immediately followed by the Route 35 bascule bridge, which only opens on the hour and half-hour, from 10 A.M. to 8 P.M., on weekends and holidays between Memorial Day and Labor Day. Following the well-marked channel for another mile brings us to the entrance of the Point Pleasant Canal, a two-mile long cut that joins the Manasquan River with the head of Barnegat Bay (chart 3.3).

Today's boaters take the extensive intracoastal waterway system for granted. But, this massive project, that made the east coast a mecca for small boat enthusiasts, was only completed in relatively recent times.

It had always been a dream of small boat skippers on the east coast to be able to travel from either New England, Long Island Sound, the Hudson River, or the Great Lakes, all the way to Florida, without ever having to cope with the open waters of the Atlantic Ocean. At the turn of the century, the increase in commercial traffic on the water as well as the heightening interest in pleasure boats, induced the state of New Jersey, and finally the federal government, to recognize the need for this inside waterway system between the mainland and the barrier islands. In 1908 New Jersey began dredging a channel inside of the barrier islands, north from Cape May. By 1915 the New Jersey section of the "Intracoastal Waterway" reached 111 miles, from Cape May to the northern end of Barnegat Bay. That same year the state obtained a right-of-way for a land cut that would extend this waterway from Bay Head, at the north end of Barnegat Bay, to the Manasquan River and Manasquan Inlet. This was originally called the Manasquan Canal and eventually came to be referred to as the Point Pleasant Canal.

From the very beginning the proposed canal was a subject of controversy. The residents at the north end of Barnegat Bay knew their fresh-water paradise would be destroyed. It would mean the fresh-water bass, bluegills, perch, and pike would cease to exist, and tides, salt water, and boat traffic would take over. In spite of this, the state kept digging until World War I forced suspension of the operation. Digging resumed after the war, and in February 1926, with appropriate ceremonies, the Manasquan River and Barnegat Bay merged.

Then something unexpected happened. Within a few months after the opening of the Manasquan Canal, the unpredictable Atlantic closed Manasquan Inlet. Of course, the canal critics blamed it on the canal, suggesting that the new waterway diverted so much water that there wasn't enough flow to keep the inlet open. They may have been right. By August, the New Jersey National Guard had managed to open a narrow channel to the ocean, but it was a losing battle and the inlet closed completely by the year 1929. Local resident David Oxenford recalls: "I can't walk on water, but I can remember, as a child, walking across Manasquan Inlet."

Chart 3.3 Manasquan Inlet and Point Pleasant Canal (reproduced from NOAA's Chart #12324)

The Point Pleasant Canal

Finally a joint county, state, and federal program was undertaken to cut through the dunes and beach and create a 400-foot wide inlet enclosed by stone jetties. The stone for these jetties came from an unlikely source. The New York subway system was being blasted out of the bedrock of Manhattan at that time, and the huge rocks were then barged down to Manasquan for the jetties. The new inlet was completed and opened in 1931.

Although the inlet worked as well as was expected, the tidal differences between the Manasquan River at the north end of the 2-mile-long canal and Barnegat Bay at the south end sometimes exceed 4 feet, creating exceptionally swift currents. Banks along the canal began to erode, and the footings of bridges were undermined. Finally, in 1935, the newly formed Bureau of Commerce and Navigation undertook the bulkheading of both sides of the canal, a project whose initial phase was finally completed in 1937.

The canal proved its worth a few years later when, during World War II, it allowed for oil barges and other commercial traffic to move inland, safe from the marauding U-boats that were hugging the New Jersey coast and the approaches to New York Harbor.

From the time of the Point Pleasant Canal's opening, the Route 88 bridge across the canal plagued boaters. More than once, boats traveling with the tide had been carried down into the closed bridge and there demolished. Boats were often unable to make way against the opposing current. This problem occured because during the height of tidal flow there was a perceptible difference in the water level on one side of the Route 88 bridge compared with the other. Only the most powerful of boats could push their way up hill, so to speak, to the other side.

There were so many problems associated with the Route 88 bridge that a new bridge was finally built, and in July 1986 it was opened for traffic. The old bridge was dismantled. At the same time, the stone shelf beneath the old bridge that had created a waterfall effect was removed. The horizontal clearance was nearly tripled, from the narrow 47 feet of the old bridge to a wide 134 feet with the new one, putting an end to one of the Point Pleasant Canal's greatest threats.

Although used frequently by small boats of all types, the canal still retains some of its early characteristics. Most powerboats have no trouble negotiating the canal at any tidal stage. Even skippers of full-powered auxiliaries should find it no problem, though they can expect a slow trip against the tide. Operators of underpowered sailboats, small outboards, or any boat with inadequate power should limit their transit to an hour or so either side of slack tide. The problem is determining when slack tide occurs. NOAA tidal current tables give the predicted time of slack water, which is, nominally, two to three hours after high or low tide in the ocean. However, times can vary greatly, depending on

Aerial view of the Point Pleasant Canal (photo courtesy of Keith Hamilton, Studio-9, Waretown)

wind conditions (direction, strength, and duration). So, determining the time of slack water is chancy at best. One bridge operator remembers that once, during an extended blow, the tide in the canal didn't change direction for three days. Compounding the tide problems is the boat traffic during weekends and holidays, which can resemble rush hour on the streets of New York.

There are two lift bridges that cross the canal. The bridgetenders can be reached on VHF Ch-13 (use low power—1 watt). The northern bridge has a clearance of 31 feet when closed and of 65 feet when open, and it responds to "Route 88 Bridge." The southern bridge has a 30-foot closed clearance and a 65-foot open clearance, and it answers to "Bridge Avenue Bridge." Both bridges open on demand, twenty-four hours a day, seven days a week. For those without VHF-FM, the standard one-long, one-short on the horn, is the alternative. Frequently, when it's obvious a sailboat needs an opening, the bridges will open without being signaled.

Long before the Point Pleasant Canal was conceived, the lifestyles of the residents at each end of the proposed waterway consisted of divergent patterns. These patterns remain in place today. On the north, the Manasquan River is host to a large commercial and recreational fishing fleet, which uses the nearby Manasquan Inlet as an access to the ocean. The water traffic here can be frenetic near the inlet on a weekend at the height of the season, as boats rush back and forth from the fishing grounds. To the south of the canal, private homes crowd the banks, and water traffic is more leisurely. The shoreline is interspersed with recreational marinas and the old boatbuilders, who made the north end of Barnegat Bay famous in the first few decades of this century. Recently, a number of these boatbuilders consolidated under single ownership. They will still build boats to custom, but they also offer the other marine services expected by transients, including repairs, marine stores, and swimming pools.

The approach to the Point Pleasant Canal from the north is at channel marker number six on the Manasquan River. The large yellow-orange brick hospital complex on the west side of the canal, at its mouth, is a landmark that's hard to miss. From the south, at Bay Head, the entrance is made with a left turn at ICW number 2, into the steel-bulkheaded waterway.

The Intracoastal Waterway provides an inland route all the way from New York City to Miami, with the exception of the 28 statute miles from Sandy Hook to the Manasquan Inlet. At one time, many boats by-passed Manasquan Inlet and took the offshore route, due to the many years of bad press about the Point Pleasant Canal. Now, with the new Route 88 bridge, there's no reason that a small boat with a draft of five feet or less shouldn't make use of the inside passage. If one combines a realistic assessment of power capabilities with a consideration of the day of the week and reasonable boating skills, this inside land cut can provide an interesting and picturesque passage—one that's much more pleasant than a trip outside in marginal weather, slugging it out with the Atlantic.

As we exit the south end of the Point Pleasant Canal, we enter the shallow waters of New Jersey's inland bays. Wandering out of the channel can mean a grounding, but the bottom is forgiving, and the greatest damage will be to one's ego.

Once on New Jersey's inside waters, boats can travel in any weather, short of a hurricane. The bay's bottom is sand and/or mud, and the Intracoastal Waterway is well marked. Late in 1991, at a cost of nearly a third of a million dollars, all buoys on the NJ-ICW were renumbered, many were eliminated, and some were changed to different types. The nine different numbering systems that were previously used for the New Jersey section of the Intracoastal have been eliminated and replaced by a single system. Now, all NJ-ICW buoys between the Point Pleasant Canal on the north and Cape May on the south have been renumbered in sequential order from north to south. This was a long-needed improvement, and in the process many buoy locations were eliminated, while other buoys were replaced with more permanent poles. Although distances between navigational aids is now greater, the new pole markers can be seen at a greater distance and will remain in place year-round (except for lighting equipment, which operates on solar-charged batteries and may be removed during the winter months). One can recognize ICW buoys because, unlike other buoys, they have a small yellow reflective panel near the buoy number.

Not only have inshore buoys been changed, but buoys at inlet entrances, as well as those at the entrance to Delaware Bay, have been changed both in number and position. If there are old charts on board, the present aids to navigation will bear no relationship in either type, number, or location to those shown on the chart.

There's a shoal area that has existed for years on the waterway near green pole-marker number 3, just after exiting the Point Pleasant Canal. Deep-draft boats should proceed with caution. Frequently, when tides are exceptionally low, the locals take the marked channel around Herring Island.

At the north end of Barnegat Bay is the appropriately-named town of Bay Head, comprised of large homes and old money. By land it is the last stop on New Jersey Transit's north Jersey coast railroad line, making it attractive to those coming from the New York City area.

The ocean trip from New York's Lower Bay, through the Manasquan Inlet and the Point Pleasant Canal is over, and it might be time to call it a day. Facilities for transients are available at one of the marinas around Bay Head or Mantoloking. If sipping cocktails and relaxing for the evening seems like a good idea, we can take a trip up the spring-fed Metedeconk River to the west. Imposing homes nestled among pine trees, private docks, yacht clubs, and marinas line the shore of this protected estuary, the name of which derives from the Lenape "Mittig-Conk," a place of good timber. As with most of New Jersey's waters that are more secluded, this 3.5-mile-long navigable channel up the wide Metedeconk is well marked with New Jersey buoys that are not shown on the federal chart. Water depth in this estuary is enough for most craft, nearly from shore to shore. On the north shore, near the western end of the Metedeconk, inside the Wehrlen Marina, is Ann's Place, a restaurant that features seafood. It is B.Y.O.B., and reservations are accepted for both slips and dinner.

The bridge across the ICW at Mantoloking (ICW mile 6.3) has a closed clearance of only 14 feet. It will only open on the hour, twenty minutes past the hour, and forty minutes past the hour, from 9 A.M. to 6 P.M., on weekends and holidays, beginning on Memorial Day and ending after Labor Day.

If we're inclined to press on a little farther south, Kettle Creek and the south shore of Silver Bay, next to the Cattus Island County Park, are attractive alternative choices as anchorages. The Cattus Island anchorage is not recommended when strong winds are from the northeast.

In central New Jersey there is an area called the Pine Barrens, 1.3 million acres of scrub pine, cedar, holly, blueberries, and cranberries. It is the largest open space between Washington, D.C., and Boston. In 1983 the United Nations designated the New Jersey Pine Barrens as an "International Biosphere Reserve." Most of the Pine Barrens, about 1.1 million acres, is protected under federal or state statutes. Just below the sandy loam of the barrens is a huge

The Mantoloking Bridge across the Intracoastal Waterway

aquifer brimming with more than 17 trillion gallons of potable water, enough to cover the entire state of New Jersey with water more than ten feet deep. Although located in the high-population density of the north-east corridor of New Jersey, the waters of this aquifer are some of the cleanest in the world. This reservoir gives birth to thousands of little brooks and streams (stained brown by tannins from the cedar trees and by iron from the soil), which wend their way leisurely into the Delaware River basin to the west or toward the tidewaters of the Atlantic shoreline to the east. Only a few fish species have adapted to these highly acidic waters. Many of these streams and creeks join in the coastal plain a few miles west of the northern end of Barnegat Bay. There, the confluence of waters becomes an estuary that continues to widen and mix with salt, until finally merging with the bay waters. This estuary is the river of Toms River, just to the west of New Jersey's Intracoastal Waterway (at ICW mile 14.5).

The mouth of Toms River is just south of the twin bridges that span the ICW and carry Route 37 highway traffic between the mainland and the barrier island. The Route 37 bridges are side by side, one fixed and the other bascule. The newer fixed bridge on the north, the J. Stanley Tunney Bridge, has a 60-foot clearance and is used for road traffic heading west. The older bascule bridge on the south, the Thomas A. Mathis Bridge, has a closed clearance of 30 feet and is used for highway traffic heading east. The bascule bridge opens only on the hour and half-hour, on weekends and holidays, between 10 A.M. and 2 P.M., from Memorial Day through Labor Day.

Passing through the Toms River bascule bridge while heading south marks a milestone, especially for sailboats. Sailboats with mast heights of under 53 feet that use the offshore route between Atlantic City and Cape May will not have to open any more bridges until the end of the cruise at Trenton. If an extended cruise south on the ICW is undertaken—one well to the south of New Jersey's waters—then the next bridge to be opened on the ICW is located just before the Dismal Swamp Canal, south of Norfolk, Virginia.

After passing under the Route 37 bridges, a trip to the west up this wide river will yield a selection of marinas or off-the-channel anchorages in a pleasant, protected atmosphere.

The channel up Toms River to the head of navigation is well buoyed, although these buoys are not shown on the chart (chart 3.4). Don't short-cut the marked channel at Long Point on the north; there is a shoal extending out from shore. The high banks along the north side of the river are dotted with many picturesque old homes, and the Toms River Yacht Club, which was founded in 1871, is one of the oldest yacht clubs in the United States.

Toms River, the county seat of Ocean County, is a historic seaport that dates back to 1624. The origin of the town's name is obscured in legend and is much

The Route 37 bridges between Toms River and Seaside Heights

debated. One version has it that the town was named after Indian Tom, a Lenape Indian who made his home on its banks. Another, more likely, story is that the name came from Captain William Tom, who visited the area frequently during the 1600s. Toms River became an important seaport after 1740, when a storm cut through the barrier island directly across from the mouth of the river, creating a wide, deep inlet to the sea. This convenient inlet led Toms River to became a major port that was strategically important during the Revolutionary War. Because of Toms River's importance, the Tories, who were loyal to the king of England, burned the town in 1782. The local populace became so infuriated that the Loyalists were forced to leave the area until the end of the war.

In 1812, the inlet that had been created in the storm of 1740, the Cranberry Inlet, closed again during another storm, and despite persistent efforts that lasted until 1850, the inlet could never be kept open for any extended period. The land south of the Cranberry Inlet then became a peninsula again, attached to the mainland, though its name, Island Beach, remained. This marked Toms River's decline as an important ocean seaport, since ships were now obliged to use the more notorious Barnegat Inlet, more than 15 miles to the south.

The creation of new inlets across the barrier islands and the closing of old ones is not uncommon. An inlet across from the Metedeconk River, Herring Inlet, and New Inlet, at the entrance to Island Beach, existed until the 1700s.

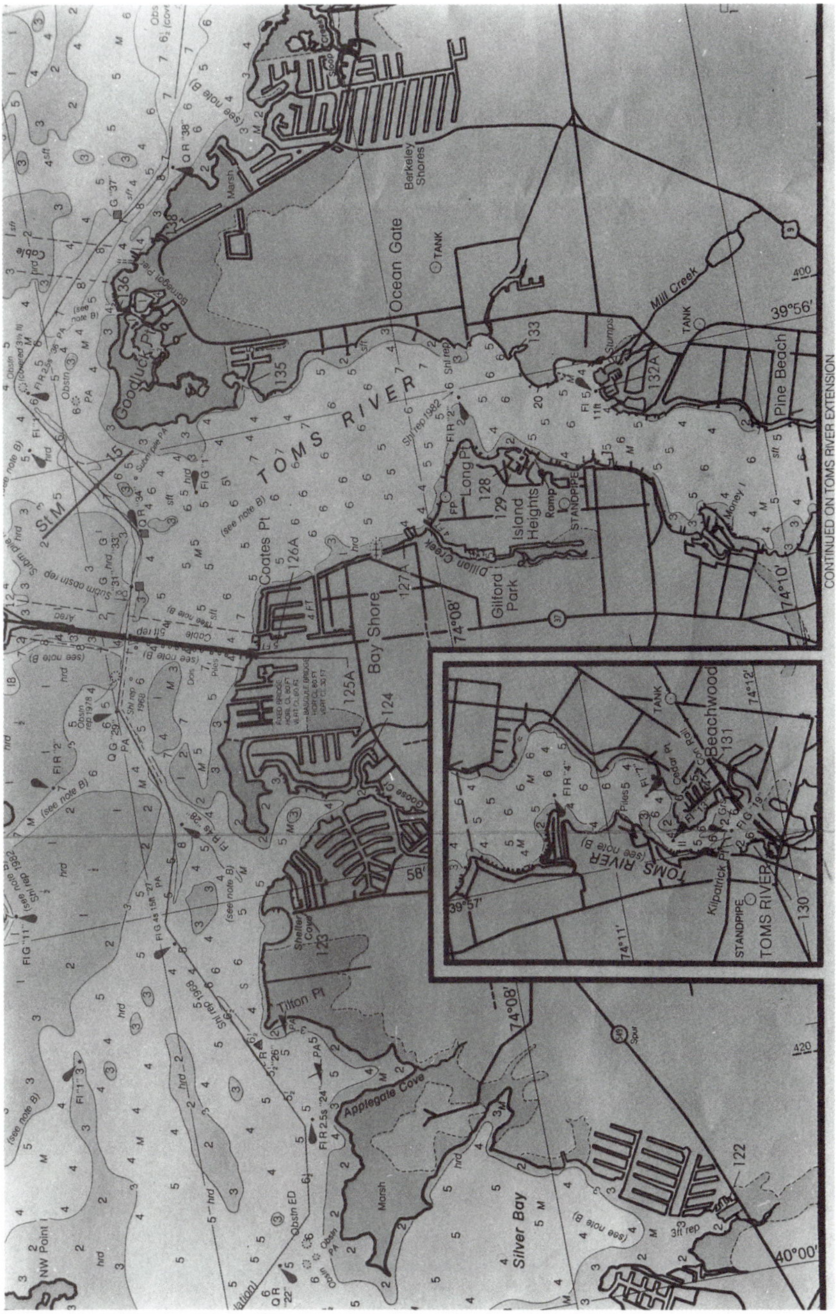

Chart 3.4 Toms River (reproduced from NOAA's Chart #12324)

Toms River

Both of these inlets were closed by the storms of 1740, when Cranberry Inlet was created. More recently, the great nor'easter of 1962 cut four new inlets across Long Beach Island. Three were rapidly closed. The fourth, a deep, broad inlet at Harvey Cedars, resisted the Army Corps of Engineers for some time, but it, too, was finally filled in.

As we travel up Toms River to the head of navigation, the waterway becomes narrower until we finally arrive in the center of town, about four miles from the mouth of the river. Many shops are within walking distance of the marinas, and The Lobster Shanty is a restaurant at the end of the river that has docks for small- to medium-sized craft or ships' tenders.

Several small coves on both sides of the river offer protected anchorages off the main channel, under the high banks of the north shore, or protected from the prevailing winds along the south shore. Toms River, even for boats of displacement-hull speeds, is less than a day's journey from Atlantic City, farther south on the NJ-ICW, or from New York City to the north.

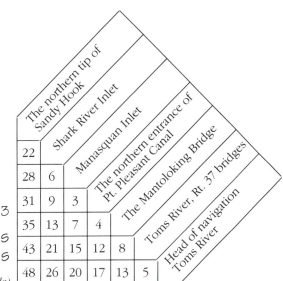

Table 3

Distances
Between Locations

(in statute miles to the nearest mile)

Chapter Four

Barnegat Bay

*S*outh of Point Pleasant there are two different New Jersey shores: the narrow barrier islands that separate the ocean from the inland tidewaters; and the wetland shore of the mainland, to the west of the Intracoastal Waterway, which snakes its way through the bays and sedges.

The main attractions for the majority of tourists visiting the New Jersey shore are the sandy beaches, the recreational activities, and the carnival atmosphere, all located on the barrier islands. While traveling to these meccas, tourists pass through the mainland shore communities with hardly a glance. However, it was the other New Jersey shore—the mainland—that attracted the first boaters to the area.

Years before Europeans came to this land, the seasonal character of New Jersey's shore was understood by the Lenape Indians, who made a yearly migration to the shore from their encampments on the bluffs of the upper Delaware River. They hiked single-file down the narrow trails that led to the coastal waters. They were the first vacationers to come to the mainland shore of Barnegat Bay, where they caught crabs, fish, clams, and oysters.

It wasn't until 1609 that Henry Hudson "discovered" the Barnegat Bay area. In his ship's log he wrote: "We came to a great lake of water . . . which was in length 10 leagues. The mouth of the lake has many shoals, and the sea breaks upon them. . . . This is a very good land to fall in with and a pleasant land to see." In spite of hundreds of years of effort and a recently completed multimillion dollar new breakwater at Barnegat Inlet, the "mouth of the lake" still "has many shoals, and the sea breaks upon them." In fact, the earliest charts of the bay differ little from today's and could still be used for navigational purposes.

For the first European settlers, the mainland side of Barnegat Bay was the most important, and few people went to the barrier islands except for hunting and whaling. During the Revolutionary War, Barnegat's sailors set out from the rivers and streams that snaked up into the desolate pinelands off the bay to attack the British ships along the coast, returning easily through the familiar inlet shoals and bars of their home waters in their shallow-draft boats. No British captain of a square-rigger would have dared follow them. The British called the area, "a nest of pirates."

By today's standards, travel in those early days was primitive. Overland routes were comprised of mud or dust in the warm months and were snow-covered or filled with frozen ruts during the winter. A trip from the Barnegat area to Philadelphia, which now takes less than two hours by car, would take two days by coastal schooner if the wind was right. It could take two weeks under adverse conditions—and there was always the possibility of never arriving at all.

When the age of the steam engine arrived, railroads began replacing the coastal schooners, and the main attraction for visitors shifted to the surf and sun on the barrier islands. In 1801, one of Long Beach Island's first boarding houses advertised rooms "for entertaining company who use sea bathing." Soon the mainland shore towns became frozen in time, by-passed by the tourists.

For the cruising sailor of today, Barnegat's shores offer many facilities for transients. There are abundant marinas, restaurants at water's edge that can be visited by boat, and stores and transportation within walking or biking distance. If a relaxed meal is part of the plan, many coves and rivers provide protected anchorages.

Nearly one-third of all of New Jersey's commercial docks, boatyards, marinas, yacht clubs, and public docks are located on both the eastern and western shores of the Barnegat Bay region. In addition, hundreds of artificially constructed lagoons and private docks provide space for private craft. The estimate is that more than 50,000 boats have immediate access to these waters. On weekends and holidays water traffic can become intimidating. Paradoxically, during summer weekdays the bay is nearly empty.

The recreational boater has always found that obtaining supplies can be a problem. A search for supplies generally leads to a marina, resulting in a detour and, usually, a docking hassle. Often, boaters find that, after all the trouble they have taken, the marina doesn't have what they need. A solution to the dilemma was introduced onto Barnegat Bay's waters in the spring of 1994, when the floating emporium, Woody's Sea Store, was launched. It operates on Barnegat Bay between Toms River and Manahawkin, the gateway to Long Beach Island.

The Sea Store, an easily identified yellow and teal houseboat, provides a wide range of sundries: cold drinks, water, ice, cigarettes, film, Sunday papers, and first-aid supplies, along with hats and sweatshirts. Its image as a country store is modified by modern services, which include telephone and FAX, as well

The Sea Store on Barnegat Bay

as 12-volt/dc-powered TV/VCRs and video cassette rentals. Cash or credit cards are accepted, and purchases are made by docking one's boat or tender alongside this floating general store.

As we travel south from Toms River into the 75 square miles of Barnegat Bay proper, we can see the ferris wheel and roller coaster at Seaside Heights, to the east. There are several marinas at Seaside, and a few slips for transients are available for the small- to medium-sized craft.

The mile-long boardwalk at Seaside Heights and the wide beaches make it a natural for kids. There are rides, pinball and video games, fast-food stands, and arcades of all kinds.

The bay near Seaside is where I had my first sail. I was eight years old, and the year was 1934. My father, who had always had the romantic notion of skippering his own sailboat, had obtained a "how-to" sail book from the library. Armed with his new-found knowledge, he took my brother and I and headed to Barnegat Bay, where he rented a catboat at Seaside Park. In the middle of the bay book learning gave way to reality, and we turned over, losing most of our clothes, all of our picnic gear, and our image of my father as a sailboat skipper. A power boat offered to pull us to shore, tied on to our bow cleat, and opened the throttle—we didn't move an inch. This was my first introduction to the

Seaside Heights, as seen from the Intracoastal Waterway

amazing holding power of a properly set anchor; ours had fallen out of the cockpit when we overturned.

It was a bedraggled group of would-be sailors that arrived home that night. When my father saw my mother in the kitchen, he said, "If we sneak in the front door, we can get upstairs before your mother sees us." It didn't work. But I had had my first sail, and I was a goner. This was for me.

When I was eleven years old I built my first boat, all by myself. It was my own design and had all the nautical lines of a coffin. It didn't last long enough to get me into any trouble, though, since the indoor plywood from which it was constructed delaminated the first season.

The second boat I built was made from a kit, a gift from my parents. I think they took pity on me. It was a wooden kayak, but I turned it into a sailboat, with a whittled-down two-by-four as a mast. My top-heavy boat could hold two very stable positions: one, with the boat on its starboard side and the mast in the water, the other on its port side, with the mast in the water. My boat was a good teacher, though, and after developing rapid reflexes, and while performing nimble feats of acrobatics, I could actually sail my boat several minutes at a time.

A quarter of a century later, I was the father, taking my son and daughter sailing on the bay. Now, sixty years after my first sail, our granddaughters are sailing with us on these same waters.

Just south of Seaside, in Berkeley Township, development on the barrier island stops. This is the north end of the 9-mile long Island Beach State Park, where rolling scrub-covered dunes, more reminiscent of Cape Cod than of the New Jersey shore, extend down to Barnegat Inlet.

Before this undeveloped beach became a state park, it had an important role during World War II. This strip of land was the site of a top-secret military project code-named Operation Bumblebee. An abandoned Coast Guard station was the base of operations for the project, which in 1945 produced the world's first successful flight of a supersonic guided missile, destined to change the face of military strategy.

After the war, when private home construction resumed, this barrier island was narrowly rescued from the decimation of bulldozers. Finally, steel magnate Henry J. Phipps, who owned Island Beach, dreamed of turning it into another Coral Gables, Florida, but after the war, in 1953, the land was purchased from his estate by the state of New Jersey and turned into a state park. A few of the original homesteaders still live on Island Beach, in homes that lack electricity, telephones, and modern conveniences, but their number is slowly diminishing.

Island Beach State Park is one of many in the Garden State. Although New Jersey is small, it has the third largest state park system in the United States.

Just to the south of the mouth of Toms River is Good Luck Point. The large brick building, surrounded by acres of masts that support transmitter antennas, is AT&T's ship-to-shore installation. Its receiving installation is a similar forest of masts farther down the bay, at Manahawkin.

On the southern tip of Good Luck Point, in the town of Bayville, just a few hundred yards off the Intracoastal at ICW Mile 16, is The Water's Edge Restaurant, which offers dining both inside and out. Thirteen slips are available for boaters, and reservations are recommended for dining but are not taken for the slips. Overnight use of the slips is not allowed. Since the restaurant's docks are adjacent to the ICW, wakes can cause problems. Many boaters anchor out and take the dinghy to the restaurant, or use the launch service that is frequently provided.

A few miles further south along the shore, also in Bayville, at ICW mile 19, Windows on the Bay is another restaurant that can be reached by boat. It offers a variety of excellent dishes and a splendid view of the bay. The dock is suitable for small- to medium-sized craft or by tenders from a large boat anchored a few hundred yards offshore, whose drafts of over two and a half feet are too deep for dockside. Reservations are a good idea on weekends or holidays.

Good Luck Point, south of the mouth of Toms River

As we continue south, Island Beach State Park encloses the bay on the east. The park is one of the last unspoiled areas along our northern Atlantic coastline. Amidst the rolling dunes are holly, bayberry, pine, beach plum, and shore grasses. Walking through the dunes on other than the fenced-in paths is prohibited.

There's a designated anchorage on the bay side of Island Beach State Park called Tices Shoal, east of ICW mile 23. It is easily identified during the summer months by the boats anchored close to shore. Here, boats with a draft of less than 5 feet can anchor in a bottom that has good holding, and the crew can swim, wade, or take a dinghy to shore and traverse the walking path across the island (about a quarter-mile) to an undeveloped ocean beach, while their boat remains safe in protected inland waters.

Some of our most cherished moments on the water have taken place when we've returned to our boat at Tices Shoal after spending a day on the beach. Supper eaten, we sit in the cockpit and watch the sun set behind the low mainland across the bay; the sky turns to shades of red and purple, and we listen to the ocean's boom and shear on the other side of the island.

Pelicans have recently migrated to this area during the summer months, and frequently, while anchored at Tices Shoal, we've seen a flock of brown pelicans

Tices Shoal, by Island Beach State Park

flying north or south along Island Beach State Park. This is a strange sight at this latitude, as they're usually seen from North Carolina south.

The waters of Barnegat Bay are home to a large number of sailboats since it affords, unlike the Chesapeake or Long Island Sound, a good sea breeze during the summer months. The legendary Jersey mosquitoes, which were troublesome a few decades ago, are now largely controlled and will only be noticeable for about an hour at sunset. The same can't be said for the aggressive greenhead fly, the bane of boaters all along the east coast. From the middle of June until September they can be a nuisance during daylight hours, mostly from Waretown south, and generally when the wind is blowing from the west out of the pine barrens. Repellents don't work well on these little monsters, and they don't mind going through heavy clothing to get their meal. Fortunately, they're only out for a limited time.

Precipitation and wind speeds are at their lowest in July, with prevailing winds from the southwest from April through August and northeast winds during September and October. Wind directions and speeds are modified by the daily sea breeze that starts in the late morning. It blows in off the ocean, created by the updraft from the warming of the mainland.

Tides on these inland waters (except when close to the inlets) run a foot or less. Of greater influence than celestial tides is the wind. Strong, prolonged west

Aerial view of Barnegat Bay; the barrier island of Island Beach State Park is in the foreground and Forked River and Waretown are across the bay on the mainland shore (photo courtesy of Keith Hamilton, Studio-9, Waretown)

winds cause very low *blow-out tides,* while onshore winds produce *blow-in tides.* This should be taken into account by skippers of deep-draft craft when they're planning an ICW cruise. During the prolonged northeast winds of the December 1992 nor'easter, blow-in tides caused the bay waters to rise higher than they have at any time in nearly fifty years, flooding many homes and businesses.

The greater Barnegat Bay area, that encompasses 47,615 acres reaching from the Toms River to the mainland town of Barnegat, is the broadest and deepest part of New Jersey's inland tidewaters (chart 4.1). Despite its location, less than one hundred miles from both New York and Philadelphia, Barnegat retains great charm. Each year ecological organizations are increasing the areas of undeveloped wetlands bordering the bay through land purchases made by the National Wildlife Preserve. Small streams extend west into the pine barrens,

Chart 4.1 Barnegat Bay (reproduced from NOAA's Chart #12323)

and the bay waters teem with crabs, clams, and fish, making it an attractive spot for the recreational boater. Ocean beaches are a short walk across the barrier island, and yacht clubs, marinas, and restaurants are just a few minutes off the ICW.

In the spring of 1992, in an effort to develop and to monitor standards for the waters of Barnegat Bay, the New Jersey Sea Grant Advisory Service initiated the Barnegat Bay Watch Monitoring Program. This program provides for the overseeing of ecological conditions in the bay, the service performed by trained citizen volunteers, who use their own boats. Equipment supplied by The Sea Grant Program and the Isaac Walton League, as well as by grants from the Victoria Foundation (a nonprofit charitable trust), and the Ciba-Geigy Corporation (the latter as a court settlement of a pollution case) enables these volunteers to record: pH levels, dissolved oxygen content, water clarity, water temperature, salinity, and precipitation. Other information collected at each station includes water depth, bottom vegetation, weather conditions, tidal stage, surface conditions, water color and odor, and wildlife observations in and on the water. The information collected by the volunteers participating in this program will provide a data-base that will aid in detecting episodic events and identifying trends or changes in water quality and habitats in the bay area.

There are many rivers, creeks, and streams that enter Barnegat Bay from the west. One of these streams, Forked River (pronounced For-ked), attracted the early settlers. After the Revolutionary War, Forked River's deep water, its "hurricane-hole" qualities, and the fact that Barnegat Inlet was across the bay, made it a natural location for coastal trading schooners and fishers, as well as for trips offshore to hunt whales. The town had food and lodging for the stage coach travelers along the sandy path that is now Route 9 and was a port of call for the coastal schooner trade. The calm bay waters, abundant with fish, crabs, and bivalves, eased the hard existence of the early settlers.

The town of Forked River has remained a flourishing fishing community, serving both recreational and commercial boaters. Its many large marinas provide access to wreck and artificial reef fishing offshore as well as to the bounties of the bay.

The river of Forked River is entered from Barnegat Bay at ICW mile 24. At center-channel tripod-shaped marker BB, which has octagon panels of vertical red and white stripes and a white light flashing Morse letter A (dot-dash), head west toward shore. There, you'll see flashing red New Jersey nun buoy number two marking the entrance to the channel that leads into the river.

At the mouth of the river, to the north, is a large expanse of wetlands, and to the south, riverside homes crowd the banks. About a mile up from the entrance, and halfway up to the head of navigation, the river separates into a south

Barnegat Bay Watch volunteers

branch. A short way up the south branch private homes are located, while farther up river, the south branch becomes the intake cooling water for the Oyster Creek Nuclear Power Plant. The warmed outlet water from the plant flows into Oyster Creek about a mile south along the bay. The 391-foot chimney

Forked River

The Oyster Creek Nuclear Power Plant

of the plant is a landmark that can be seen far up and down the ICW. Residents of the area seem to coexist comfortably with the nuclear plant, which pays a large portion of the local taxes.

As we travel a little further up the north fork, the middle fork branches off to the south and is flanked by private homes and docks. The north fork provides all of the facilities of interest to transients: ten marinas with gas and diesel, repair service, haul-out facilities, pump-out stations, private and public launching ramps, and slips for transients.

A restaurant popular with both local boaters and transients, The Captain's Inn, is located on this north fork. The inn has many guest slips (white pilings) that are seldom filled, even on weekends or holidays. Showers are available, and transients can remain in a guest slip overnight.

At the head of navigation (about 2 miles from the bay), is the 181-slip Forked River State Marina. It was built as a WPA project in the 1930s. There you'll find a recently completed new marina building with showers and laundry. In the spring of 1994 the state announced its intention of putting the marina up for sale, and on December 15, 1994, the marina was auctioned off for $900,000. Several legal issues surrounding the sale needed to be ironed out. The final transfer was scheduled for September of 1995. This privatization will undoubtedly lead to higher fees for slips and services, since the State Division of

The Captain's Inn on Forked River

Parks and Forestry, which operated the marina, did not have to pay local property taxes.

The marinas along Forked River's north fork are located on or near the major north/south artery of Route 9, providing access to buses that head south to Atlantic City and Cape May or north to northern New Jersey and New York City. This makes it a convenient spot for picking up or discharging passengers. From these marinas it is a short walk or bike ride to a marine-supply store, restaurants, a laundromat, drug stores, food stores, the library, a motel, banks with ATMs, bait and fishing suppliers, ice machines, churches, and a variety of other stores and services located along Route 9.

For most of this century the area west of Barnegat Bay remained rural, and the natives were called *pineys,* a term that is considered a badge of honor by the old-time residents. Recently, many new expensive homes have been built on the local waterways, slowly changing the character of the area. Almost gone are the days of the commercial fisher, which are giving away to the recreational boater.

Sometimes the old-timers view the recent changes ruefully. Several years ago I was sitting in the old garvey of a weather-beaten and bearded piney clammer. The paint on the hull of the boat was peeling, and the hardware was weeping rust. The grooves in the rails attested to many years of wear from a

Aerial view of Forked River looking down the river from the head of navigation (photo courtesy of Keith Hamilton, Studio-9, Waretown)

clam rake. We watched as the commissioning ceremonies of a newly-built yacht club got under way. "Them fellows gets all dressed up in them white uniforms," the clammer muttered, "but they don't know nothin' 'bout the water."

Each year, it seems, there are fewer of the honest old wooden work boats that, for centuries, have wrestled a livelihood from the bay and the sea.

At the mouth of Forked River, the ICW is just outside the entrance buoys,

A clammer at work on Barnegat Bay

but if we're ready to spend the night at anchor, or if we're just interested in a peaceful lunch break or supper on board, we go along the undeveloped wetland shores just north of the river and drop the hook. Traveling south close to shore will put us aground; there's an underwater sandbar there. Near the wetlands the water runs 5 to 6 feet deep, almost to shore, and we are protected from west winds. If we're inclined, we might want to try fishing or crabbing. Harvesting clams or other mollusks from New Jersey's waters requires a license, and shellfish cannot be taken in condemned waters, from leased grounds, or on Sunday.

In the bays all along New Jersey's coastline the blue-claw crab is pursued by both commercial and recreational crabbers, and small wonder since, although this crab is always pugnacious, it is always delicious. All you need are some weighted handlines (with fish heads or chicken necks for bait), a net, and a basket, and you're ready for a fresh seafood treat. Don't fail to throw back crabs that are less than the legal width (four and a half inches point-to-point across the shell for recreational crabbers, as of March 1994) and females with eggs (visible as reddish roe clinging to the crab's underside).

In addition, there are, of course, seasonal, size, and number restrictions on several of the fish species in both the bay and the ocean. Contact the Marine Fisheries Administration or a bait store for more information.

Long before European settlers adopted Barnegat Bay's waters as their own, Native Americans used the bay as a nearly unlimited source of food.

In 1609, the Indians who camped along these shores had their first view of Europeans and their strange ships.

In September of that year, Henry Hudson anchored his ship, *The Half Moon*, in the ocean just outside Barnegat Inlet and sent a longboat through the inlet on an exploration mission into Barnegat Bay. On their return, the sailors reported seeing a sea monster in the bay. (It must have been a very shoal-draft sea monster.) The sea monster was described in the log of *The Half Moon*, where it was said to possess "three humps and a snake's head," and was seen "moving at the speed of a small boat." The sea monster wasn't seen again until 1935, when two fishermen anchored in the bay near Forked River photographed it; there is some question as to the photo's authenticity.

I can nearly guarantee, based on years of experience, that boaters cruising the bay will not be molested by sea monsters.

The busy Oyster Creek Channel, opposite Waretown, joins the ICW on Barnegat Bay with Barnegat Inlet and the town of Barnegat Light. The juncture of Oyster Creek Channel and the ICW on Barnegat Bay had been marked for decades by green can-buoy number 67. With the implementation of the new buoy system, late in 1991 this marker was removed, and a red-and-white vertical-striped pole, marker BI, now indicates this juncture. This new *safe water* marker is mounted on a *dolphin* (a cluster of pilings lashed together) and has a white light flashing Morse letter A (dot-dash).

For the transient who is unfamiliar with Oyster Creek Channel, a brief description will be helpful. The channel heads east from the juncture marker BI, and although well marked, navigational aids are uncharted. There's no room for error here. The channel is narrow, with shoals on both sides. Dog-leg turns in the channel can be overlooked and, when properly executed, they can bring the boat broadside to the tidal flow—so looking over one's shoulder to line up the course is the rule. Every day during the summer we see someone aground outside the channel, waiting for a change of tide. The aerial photo of Oyster Creek Channel should provide enough information to warrant caution.

Well before arriving at Barnegat Light, the Oyster Creek channel passes close to the south of several large sedges, which have been the site of a hunting lodge since before the turn of the century. The lodge's excellent duck hunting and companionship attracted many notables at the time, including John D. Rockefeller, Jr., and his wife Abby, and Babe Ruth, who enjoyed making clam chowder for the crowd at the nightly poker game. The building can be easily seen from Oyster Creek Channel.

After the passage through the tortuous twists, turns, and shoals, we arrive

Aerial view of Oyster Creek Channel, which joins Barnegat Inlet with Barnegat Bay and the Intracoastal Waterway (photo courtesy of Keith Hamilton, Studio-9, Waretown)

next at Barnegat Lighthouse. Here the channel to the south takes us to the docks at the town of Barnegat Light, on Long Beach Island, where marinas and an anchorage are convenient to both Barnegat Inlet and an offshore passage.

The channel heading north, out of Barnegat Inlet, takes us past the lighthouse, which is no longer navigational and only shows a token light. The lighthouse was reopened to visitors in 1991, after extensive repairs, and is well worth the climb up its 217 steps. There's a 32-acre state park surrounding the lighthouse; it's open to the public and offers picnic facilities, bathrooms, fishing in the inlet, and the opportunity to climb the lighthouse. The wire screen around the open platform at the top of the lighthouse helps prevent accidents, but its primary function is to eliminate the costly glass replacement on the dome, as migrating ducks and geese frequently crash into the tower at night.

There are restaurants and limited supplies, as well as the ocean beach, within walking distance of Barnegat Light's marinas.

For those who would prefer to anchor out, or for transients who enter through Barnegat Inlet to lay over for the night, there is an anchorage basin just

Barnegat Lighthouse

to the southwest of the lighthouse, with adequate water for deep-keel craft. It is a protected anchorage in nearly all wind conditions, with moderate tidal flow, and it's a convenient spot to spend the night in anticipation of an early morning departure.

The first Barnegat Lighthouse was built in the dunes far from the inlet in 1834 and was illuminated by oil. Since New Jersey inlets have a tendency to migrate south, the lighthouse soon stood at the edge of the inlet and finally collapsed into the water in 1856. Construction on a new lighthouse (the present one) was started in 1857 and was completed a year later. Its walls are ten feet thick at the base and eighteen inches thick at the top, and the windows along the spiral staircase face different points of the compass. The original lens, made in France, weighed 5 tons, yet it could be turned by the pressure of one finger. It was rotated by a 150 lb. weight on sixty-five feet of rope inside the newel column of the spiral staircase, and it had to be wound up to the top every hour. When constructed, it was the second tallest lighthouse in the U.S.A. (The tallest was located in Pensacola, Florida.)

On August 15, 1927, the lighthouse was replaced by a lightship anchored offshore. The lightship couldn't be seen from any further out at sea than had the lighthouse, and it required a fourteen-man crew in comparison to the three men who had been assigned to the lighthouse—a major step forward in efficiency.

An unusual event took place in 1951, when the lightship presented the Coast Guard with an unsolved mystery. After a May nor'easter, it was discovered that the heavy anchor chain had tied itself into a perfect overhand knot halfway between the anchor and the lightship. There was never any explanation, even from the Coast Guard, which only went so far as to explain in its "Coast Guard Bulletin": "The anchor at one end of the chain weighs a ton or more. The ship, of course, is attached to the other."

Lighthouse, lightships, and buoys have marked the entrance to Barnegat Inlet for over a century and a half, and the attempts to keep the inlet navigable have continued from then to the present time.

The three-year, multimillion dollar reconstruction and realignment of the south jetty of Barnegat Inlet was completed in 1991. This project represents an attempt to deepen and stabilize the inlet, which has always been considered one of the most dangerous on the east coast. The newly finished south jetty juts out nearly a half mile into the ocean and, unlike the old south jetty, is parallel to the north jetty. The area between the old and new south jetties is now a huge sand bar. The design anticipates that the new jetty will create a flushing action that will deepen and maintain the inlet, a spot that has been notorious for its shallow entrance and breaking seas.

It is too soon to be sure that the new jetty will bring about the desired results. The government has been fixing Barnegat Inlet ever since I was a child, but the inlet's nature has always been unstable and perverse. Even with the completion of this new jetty, it would be wise to use this inlet with caution until its new character is known and, then, only when conditions are ideal. It is always easier to exit through the inlet than it is to enter. Steep seas build up near the mouth and, at low tide, even on relatively calm days, breakers can be encountered. The new inlet configuration will be shown only on the latest of charts.

Aerial view of Barnegat Inlet, Oyster Creek Channel, and Barnegat Bay. The Oyster Creek Nuclear Plant is on the mainland in the distance (photo courtesy of Keith Hamilton, Studio-9, Waretown)

Another channel that joins Barnegat Inlet to the bay is located at a point farther south on ICW, at mile 28, near marker 42. This is Double Creek Channel; its twists and turns are marked but not charted. There are several shoal areas in the channel near the inlet, and it shouldn't be used at low tide by any boat with a draft of more than 2.5 feet.

On the mainland shore, in Waretown, one will find The Doc's Place restaurant at the Cape Island Marina. To visit the restaurant, take the entrance channel to the south of the large marina/restaurant building at water's edge. Slips for the restaurant are located just beyond the fuel dock and also around the corner to the right.

Due south of ICW marker number 42, next to the shore of Conklin Island, there is a good anchorage for a meal aboard, a swim off the boat, or a quiet overnight stay, where the waters are protected from the prevailing south and west winds, but not from winds issuing from the northern quadrant. There is good holding here in a muddy sand bottom.

Just to the west of this anchorage is the marked but uncharted channel that leads into the mainland town of Barnegat. Several marinas, which provide a complete range of services, are just off the channel beyond the town dock and are identified by the two-story open gazebo. A forest of masts identifies the largest of these, Mariner's Marina, which nearly always has slips for transients, and offers a ship's store; a travel-lift; and a full range of repair services for hull, engine, and rigging. The center of the quaint old town of Barnegat is a long walk or a short bike ride away (about one mile), and a supermarket is in the other direction, on Bay Avenue, a two mile ride from the marinas. The marina office provides telephone numbers for Chinese food and for pizza that can be delivered right to the marina, as well as information about restaurants within walking distance.

Throughout all of New Jersey's tidal waters there are opportunities for the curious cruiser to find interesting and protected *gunkholes*. Those new to boating are probably unfamiliar with this word, and it is one they can't find in most dictionaries. It is common usage in the lexicon of the inveterate cruiser, however, and can be used as either a noun or a verb. Gunkholing is the exploration of shallow, nearly unnavigable, and unmarked waterways and coves in search of seclusion, adventure, or wildlife.

From the wide expanses of Barnegat Bay, we'll now head further south on the ICW, through the narrow, shallow, and twisting waterway that leads to Atlantic City.

Chapter Five

The Intracoastal Waterway Between Barnegat Bay and Atlantic City

*A*lthough most of New Jersey's coastal residents use the name Barnegat Bay as an all-inclusive name to denote the waters from Bay Head to Beach Haven, Barnegat Bay comes to an end south of the mainland town of Barnegat. The bay waters between this point and the southern end of Long Beach Island have the separate names of Manahawkin Bay and Little Egg Harbor.

To the south of Barnegat Inlet, the eighteen-mile long stretch of land, Long Beach Island, is a family-oriented resort—no high rises here. There are many yacht clubs and marinas off the ICW, all along the bay side of Long Beach Island. From these facilities, it is a short walk to stores, entertainment, restaurants, or to spend a day on the oceanfront. Here, as on most of New Jersey's barrier-island beaches, beach badges (for a fee) are required when life guards are on duty, from Memorial Day to Labor Day. These badges can usually be obtained at the local municipal building or from the badge patrol on the beach; they can be purchased for the season, the week, or the day (and are frequently free to senior citizens). Rules for each beach, specifying those activities that are prohibited, are generally posted on a sign at the entrance path to the beach.

Water sports of all kinds exist on both the bay side and ocean side of the barrier islands and include: swimming, jet skiing, sailing, wind surfing, snorkeling, surfing, scuba diving, water-skiing, fishing, crabbing, clamming, and motorboating.

Many residents of southern New Jersey, from Long Beach Island south, are fond of telling people that they live below the Mason-Dixon line. The east-west portion of that line was established at latitude 39°43.325', and if it had extended through New Jersey, it would have crossed Long Beach Island just south of

The Atlantic Coast Championship for the snipe class at Surf City Yacht Club on Manahawkin Bay. The Yacht Clubs on Long Beach Island host regattas and championships for many classes of small sailboats, with participants from all over the United States and occasionally foreign countries.

Loveladies. The southern part of New Jersey is south of that latitude, but the line itself, the boundary between Pennsylvania and Maryland (established by surveyors Charles Mason and Jeremiah Dixon), was never extended through the Garden State.

Although it is speculated that Sebastian Cabot, an English navigator, may have been the first European to see Long Beach Island, there is very little documentation of his voyage.

It appears that he explored the coast of North America from the Delmarva Peninsula north, in 1498, on a futile voyage to discover the northwest passage, and it's likely his explorations included the coast of New Jersey.

Giovanni da Verrazano was more probably the first European to see New Jersey's barrier islands, when he was on his way north along the coast in 1524. These narrow strips of land are characteristic of much of the Atlantic seaboard and the Gulf coast from Manasquan, New Jersey, to the Mexican border.

In 1617, three years before the *Mayflower* pilgrims landed on Plymouth Rock, the Dutch were establishing colonies in the Barnegat Bay area. Whaling along the shores of Long Beach Island began in the mid-1600s. To aid whalers, a crow's nest was erected on the beach and used as a lookout. When whales were spotted, either ships in the bay exited the inlets for the chase or boats were launched through the surf after the prey. When these surf-launched boats killed the whale, it was towed back to shore, cut up, and rendered on the beach.

Although Long Beach Island has been used by hunters, fishers, and whalers, even before the arrival of the Europeans, it could only be reached by boat until just over a century ago, when train service was begun. The railroad arrived at Long Beach Island in 1886. The low trestle across the bay at Manahawkin was frequently covered by storm tides and, finally, in the nor'easter of 1935, it was washed away and never rebuilt. The first road to the island, also a low causeway just a few feet above the water and parallel to the railroad bridge, was built in 1914 and remained in service until it was replaced in 1959. Now, a high, arching fixed bridge, with a 60-foot clearance, links Ship Bottom on the island with Manahawkin on the mainland. Tens of thousands of vacationers pour over this bridge during the summer months to enjoy the island's relaxed atmosphere and clean beaches. It is the only land link to the island.

Boats that cruise the waters inside the barrier islands are almost completely safe from the vagaries of weather—almost, but not quite. Fortunately, hurricane

The ocean beach on Long Beach Island

and tropical storm forecasts now alert us well in advance and allow those on the water plenty of time for preparation. Not so with summer thunderstorms, during which winds can sometimes reach hurricane velocity and occur with little advance warning.

We have been on board sailboats during hundreds of thunderstorms, mostly when cruising the Caribbean and the southeastern states, and we've even been on the water when as many as three waterspouts were just a few miles away (while sailing on the ocean side of the Florida Keys). However, our most violent experience in a thunderstorm took place in those benign, protected waters of New Jersey's inland bays, in Little Egg Harbor, off Long Beach Island.

We had anchored in the bay for a rendezvous with our friend John Fider, who tied his Sunfish to our stern and joined us for lunch on board. Just as we were finishing lunch the sky became dark and the wind shifted 180°, a bad sign. We could hear the rumble of thunder over the mainland, and as John checked the line on his Sunfish, we let out more scope on the anchor and closed the ports and hatches. Suddenly John extended his arm and in a near-whisper said, "Look at that!" Across the bay the water had turned into a white froth as the squall line raced toward us. We all retreated into the cabin except for John, who wanted to experience the adventure in the cockpit. Then it hit.

We heard a large snap, and the boat went over 90°, the top of the mast hitting the water. A tiny exposed section of our roller-furling Genoa jib had been grabbed by the wind, the huge sail unrolling to its fullest, knocking the boat over on its beam's end. As our son Tom and I struggled out of the cabin, the boat righted itself to about 45°. John was not in the cockpit.

The lightning and thunder were simultaneous and, as we searched for John, the lightning flashes all around us were like glowing trees in the sky. The mixture of rain and hail, driven by the hurricane force winds, felt painful, even through our clothes. Finally, we heard John calling from behind the boat. I dropped the sail in the water, while Tom helped John back on board.

John later told us that when the wind hit, his Sunfish became airborne at the end of its tether and spun around three times, with the mast slashing through the water on each revolution. When our boat turned over, John couldn't hold on and fell out of the cockpit, but he managed to grab on to his Sunfish.

We discovered later that the anemometer at the Brant Beach Yacht Club nearby registered seventy-five miles an hour—hurricane force winds. Boats were overturned and, on shore, shingles were ripped from roofs and doors were torn from their hinges.

When the squall passed we assessed our damage. Surprisingly, our boat was intact, with no damage and no water in the cabin. The Sunfish had lost its daggerboard and life jacket, and the mast, a heavy three-inch aluminum extrusion, was bent. We counted our blessings.

In sixty years on the water I had never experienced such a thunderstorm and, hopefully, I never will again. That night John and I spliced the main brace—and you can imagine how well we spliced it. So, let this be a caveat for anyone who ventures out on the water: don't take the weather for granted, even on the so-called protected waters inside of the barrier islands.

Long ago, when the Europeans first began settling along the shores of Little Egg Harbor, the area was sparsely populated by Native Americans. The forests were home to deer, wolves, panthers, bobcats, bear, turkeys, quail, and pheasant. Cranberries, grapes, and nuts grew wild. The shallow waters of the bay abounded in crabs, clams, oysters, and numerous fish and waterfowl.

The Lenape Indians introduced the original Quaker settlers to foods unknown in Europe—more than forty in all, including pumpkins, kidney and lima beans, corn, tomatoes, potatoes, and squash. The New Jersey Lenapes were an agrarian tribe and were skilled at fertilizing and rotating crops. Every fall they held a festival of thanks to their god Manitou for the harvest bestowed on them. The pilgrims adopted this tradition, calling it Thanksgiving. The Quakers were appreciative of the bountiful land and were on friendly terms with the American Indians, whom they paid for the land they used.

Although that era is but a history-book memory, changes over the centuries have gently touched these intracoastal waters. As we continue our cruise through Little Egg Harbor, our modern charts differ little from the charts first drawn by the early settlers.

As we continue our cruise south on Little Egg Harbor, past the scene of our frightening experience, we near the southern end of Long Beach Island and the town of Beach Haven. There are large marinas and yacht clubs just off the ICW, along the southern end of the island. Here, there is access to shopping, restaurants, amusements, and the ocean beach, a short walk away. Beach Haven is the busiest and most densely populated town on the island. During the summer there is a large generation-X population (adults in their twenties and thirties), and in the evening the neighborhood bars are jumping. But, there are plenty of attractions for the kids too. Fantasy Island, on West 17th Street, is a huge amusement park that provides entertainment for children of all ages.

On the ICW, at Beach Haven, at red, flashing marker LB, there is a channel that leads into the deepest part of Little Egg Harbor and that connects the ICW with Tuckerton on the mainland. Old-time shipboard radio operators from the first half of this century remember the high-seas transmitting and receiving station at Tuckerton to be one of their few reliable links to the mainland.

The tower that provided this service was constructed by a German radio company, which began building in 1912, on Hickory Island off Tuckerton. The site was chosen for its firm ground, its unimpeded transmission of radio waves out to the Atlantic and toward Europe, and its soil, which was saturated with salt water and acted as an ideal radio-frequency ground plane. The 853-foot tower was completed in 1914 (just at the beginning of World War I), and it was the second highest construction in the world, next to the Eiffel Tower. Its intended purpose was trans-Atlantic communications as well as ship-to-shore service, and it was taken out of German management when the United States entered into World War I.

Tuckerton has a history, going back for three centuries, that belies the size of this small rural town. Its easy access to the nearby inlets, its protected water-way, and its proximity to mainland transportation, thrust it into importance even before the birth of our country.

Tuckerton, originally called Quakertown, then Fishtown, and finally Clam-town, was renamed after the Revolution by Ebenezer Tucker. Tucker was a member of Congress, who used his political clout to establish Tuckerton as the third port of entry into the new nation in 1791, under a commission from George Washington.

In commemoration of Tuckerton's past, plans are now underway to create an historical seaport complex at the head of Tuckerton Creek, near the center of town, just off Route 9.

Although no longer a port of entry, Tuckerton's proximity to the Intracoastal Waterway and to Little Egg Inlet makes it a convenient home port for recreational craft.

There are numerous facilities for shoal-draft boats on the north side of the approach channel, at the entrance to Tuckerton Creek, as well as in the creek itself, where there is approximately two and a half feet of water at low tide for a mile and a half upstream. Tuckerton Creek has had various names. The American Indians called it Pohatcong, and in the early 1700s it was known as An-drews' Mill Creek, then Shourds' Mill Creek, Mill Creek, and finally, Tuckerton Creek.

Tuckerton possesses the only museum dedicated to the history, traditions, and skills of the New Jersey "baymen." The Barnegat Bay Decoy and Baymen's Museum was opened in 1993. Displays include more than 150 decoys, an antique sneakbox, a Seabright skiff, and artifacts of the 19th and 20th centuries that were used for oystering, clamming, fishing, hunting, collecting salt hay, and life saving. It is located about a quarter of a mile south on Route 9 from the head of navigation on Tuckerton Creek.

Back on the Intracoastal Waterway, we head south past the southern tip of

Chart 5.1 The twin inlets of Beach Haven and Little Egg (reproduced from NOAA's Chart #12316)

Long Beach Island, where the ICW passes inside of the twin inlets of Beach Haven and Little Egg (chart 5.1). Strong winds from the southeast can send high waves through these inlets and across the inland waterway, making the trip uncomfortable or even dangerous for small boats. For centuries the shoreline in this area has experienced drastic changes, and these changes continue. There are constantly shifting shoals within the inlets and along this exposed section of the ICW, especially after a storm. The ICW buoys in this area are frequently relocated and may not correspond to even the newest of charts.

When heading either north or south, don't confuse the buoys of Marshelder Channel, which leads toward Tuckerton, with those of the ICW. This can easily put you on a shoal, so newcomers should check the chart in this area meticulously.

The September 1992 edition of the chart shows a shoal directly across the waterway between ICW markers 114 and 116. This can be a source of confusion, but note that the magenta line that indicates the ICW does, in fact, cross over this shoal area. Owners of deep-draft craft would be wise to negotiate this leg with caution, and preferably on a rising tide.

As the ICW makes a right-angle turn to the west into Great Bay, the cupola on the chart at Shooting Thoroughfare indicates a building that was formerly a Coast Guard station and now houses the Center for Coastal Environment Studies for the Marine Science Center of Rutgers University. The building, which still retains the white siding and red roof of a Coast Guard station, is built on the low wetlands that, at high tide, frequently flood the land beneath the building and often make Great Bay Boulevard, which is the only access road, impassable. With funds from recent grants, improvements and expansion projects are under way at this facility that will provide high-tech ecosystem monitoring equipment as well as additional trained personnel.

At marker 132, a shoal has developed out into the waterway for thirty or forty feet, with water just a few inches deep at low tide; so don't hug this pole too closely.

Farther south, the ICW travels a small distance through the southeast corner of Great Bay. The channels here tend to shoal and change, and those in boats drawing over four feet should try to make the trip to Atlantic City on a rising tide. The waterway is especially narrow as it passes west of Tow Island, and staying in center channel is a must. Once we met on-coming traffic here, and when cheating toward the edge of the waterway but while still inside of the markers, we ran aground. In late 1994 approval was granted for dredging about a third of a mile along this section of the ICW, which should improve the situation, at least temporarily.

An interesting gunk hole can be found on a side trip up the Mullica River,

The Marine Science Center of Rutgers University

whose entrance is in the northwest corner of Great Bay and is considered to be one of the cleanest and least disturbed estuaries in the Boston to Washington, D.C., corridor.

Around the middle of the seventeenth century, Swedish immigrant Eric Mullica established a community along the Little Egg Harbor River and laid claim to a large parcel of land. Little Egg Harbor River can't be found on charts; it is now known as the Mullica River.

The Mullica is rich in history. The iron bogs along its shores supplied Washington's army with cannon balls during the Revolution. This bog-iron ore, a hydrous peroxide of iron, was refined in huge charcoal kilns and was for years the chief industry in this part of southern New Jersey. Several miles up the Mullica River, Bass River branches off north, where there are small-craft facilities on both sides of the river in the small town of New Gretna (just before the 9-foot bascule bridge on Route 9 and the 20-foot fixed bridge on the Garden State Parkway).

There are five major boat companies that build powerboats in this part of the Garden State. Viking, Egg Harbor, Post Marine, Silverton, and Ocean Yachts are all within twenty-five miles of each other (the large Pacemaker Company, which was also part of this group, is now defunct).

New Gretna is the home of the Viking Yacht Company, the state's largest boat builder. The company is now experiencing a recovery, after the ill-conceived ten percent tax on luxury boats (in conjunction with a sagging economy) nearly shut down the boat-building industry before its repeal in 1993. Viking's work force, which was 1,500 before the tax, dropped to around 60 within a year after its passage. Viking's Bass River Township plant manufactures fiberglass motor yachts, ranging from thirty-eight to sixty-six feet and averaging $750,000 each.

Egg Harbor Yachts is located in Egg Harbor City; Silverton, in Millville; Ocean Yachts, in Weekstown. Other boat-builders in New Jersey include Post Marine, in Mays Landing; Henriques Boat Works, in Bayville; and Cherubini Boat Company, in Delran.

One can gunkhole to the other tributaries of the Mullica: Nacote Creek, 4 miles from the Mullica's mouth, has about five feet of water to the bascule bridge on Route 9, and then three feet to Port Republic; Wading River, 7.5 miles up the Mullica, has a water depth of about four feet to the bascule span at Route 542 (chart 5.2).

In addition to the marinas and boatyards on Bass River in New Gretna, there is a marina on the Mullica River, about a half mile before the Garden State Parkway's 30-foot fixed bridge, and another further upriver. There are also facilities on Nacote Creek, just before the Route 9 bridge.

An interesting trip can be made up the Mullica to the head of navigation at Sweetwater. It is a trip that's popular with local boaters whose craft draw less than three feet and have mast heights that will clear the Garden State Parkway's 30-foot fixed bridge. This part of the Mullica is beyond the limits of the government chart #12316, but the channel is marked all the way to the fork in the river before Batsto. The charming inn, The Fork's, is located near the last channel marker. About a half mile before The Fork's one will find the Sweetwater Casino, another popular restaurant. Both eateries usually have dock space available, and fuel can be obtained at the Sweetwater Casino's fuel dock or further down the river, near the bascule bridge.

There are two bascule bridges between Great Bay and the restaurants at Sweetwater. The first, 13 miles up the river from its mouth, on Route 652, has a closed clearance of 6 feet, and the second, 3 miles further up, on Route 563, has a 5-foot closed clearance.

This side excursion up the Mullica is representative; there are many interesting possibilities for exploration that exist on the hundreds of rivers, creeks, and streams wending their way off the beaten track into the New Jersey wetlands and uplands. It would take a separate book to cover all of these navigable streams.

After this sojourn and back on the ICW, we will be able to see the tall

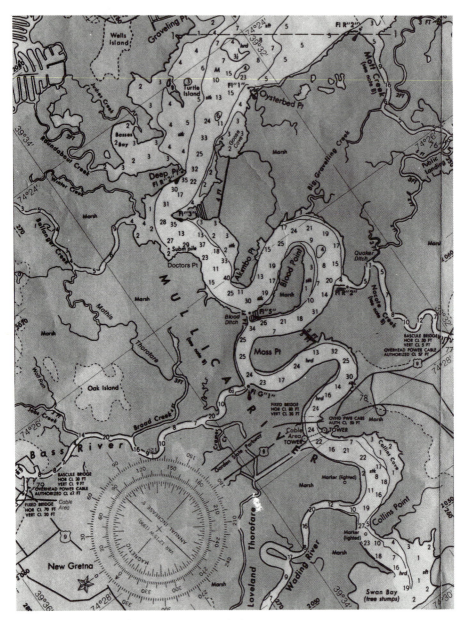

$\mathcal{C}$hart 5.2 The Mullica, Bass, and Wading rivers (reproduced from NOAA's Chart #12316)

buildings of Atlantic City across the wetlands of the Forsythe National Wildlife Refuge at Brigantine (when the weather is clear). Refuge lands scattered along the shores of the bays comprise more than 39,000 acres of wetlands, making it the largest National Wildlife Refuge in the northeast region (thirteen states, from

The upper reaches of the Mullica River at Sweetwater

Canada to North Carolina), second only to the Great Dismal Swamp of Virginia and North Carolina. The Forsythe refuge is the home of a remarkable variety of shore birds and raptors, as well as to the diverse waterfowl of the Atlantic flyway, wintering some thirty-five percent of the flyway's black duck population and nearly seventy percent of its Atlantic brants. The United Nations has listed the Forsythe habitat as one among only four sites in the U.S. originally included in its Wetlands of International Importance program.

Each year environmental organizations, in conjunction with the government, acquire new parcels of wetlands in an effort to preserve those last tracts of undeveloped shoreline. This effort is spearheaded by the Izaak Walton League, which relies on contributions and the Trust for Public Land for funding.

The TPL is a private, nonprofit conservation organization that works nationally to protect open space for people and wildlife. The TPL purchases endangered parcels and holds them temporarily until they can be resold to a government agency. This saves the government a tremendous amount of work and allows for effective use of the limited public money available. Once a refuge is established, the U.S. Fish and Wildlife Service (part of the Department of the Interior) is the governmental organization that oversees its operation.

Often on our cruises, we delve into our onboard library to read the history of the area we're passing through or to identify wildlife and waterfowl. From a

The docks at the Fork's Inn, near the head of navigation on the Mullica River

lifetime of cruising these waters, we are able to identify most of the species, but occasionally we're surprised by one that is unfamiliar.

On our southward path, the ICW cuts through the center of the Forsythe Refuge, a bird watcher's delight. From the standpoint of bird-watching, early spring and fall are the best times for this trip, since the refuge is inhabited by huge numbers of migratory fowl. This is also the best time if one is concerned about creature comforts. During the summer months, in a slow boat, and with the wind from the west, a trip through this area can be daunting. It is the policy of the refuge not to interfere with the natural procreation of any of the wildlife, including greenhead flies, and they can be a nuisance to summertime bird watchers or to Atlantic City-bound gamblers. The only worse case of greenhead flies we've encountered plagued us when we were traveling the ICW through the Georgia savannas. My wife, Elsie, closed herself in the cabin while I did a swatting dance in the cockpit. I was itching to get away from there.

Nearly midway through the Forsythe refuge, a channel branches off the ICW to the east, which gives access to the shore town of Brigantine. Here, one will find a half dozen small marinas with fuel and supplies. This channel is extremely narrow in spots—at times only 15 or 20 feet—and at the edge of the

The Forsythe Refuge, with Atlantic City in the distance

channel there is no water at all. If a visit by boat to Brigantine is on the schedule, it is best to use the channel further to the south; the entrance is just west of Atlantic City and opposite buoy number 178.

In Atlantic City itself, there are three major marinas available to the recreational transient (chart 5.3). The largest is the Senator Frank S. Farley Marina, a public facility owned by the New Jersey Division of Parks and Forestry and managed by Trump's Castle Associates. It is located in Clam Creek Basin, just off the south side of the inlet, and has 640 slips (474 seasonal and 166 for transients), with 8 feet of water at dockside. Slips have shore power, water, telephone, and cable TV, and floating docks make getting on and off the boat much easier. Contact with the dock master is via VHF Ch-65. The slips are easy to enter and have the advantage of not being affected by the tidal flow. Gas, diesel, and a pump-out station are available, along with a waste-oil disposal station, showers, laundry, a health club, miniature golf, a jogging track, tennis courts, winter bubbler system, picnic areas, coupons for free buffet breakfasts, and 24-hour security. All are included in the $1.25/foot/day slip fee. There is also a marina store that carries boating supplies and nautical clothing and gifts. It also has a convenience-store section. The Harbor View Restaurant, a snack bar, and The Captain's Lounge are located in the marina building. Across the road, which

The Sen. Frank S. Farley State Marina in Atlantic City (photo courtesy of Trump's Castle Associates)

is accessible by a covered walkway, is Trump's Castle (with casinos, restaurants, hotel accommodations, and shops). A jitney stop is located on the street between Trump's Castle and the marina building.

The jitney is Atlantic City's answer to San Francisco cable cars. Jitneys are available from the marinas to any of the twelve casinos; there is also a two-mile ride to the boardwalk, eliminating the long walk through areas that are considered unsafe. The price for a jitney ride is about one-sixth of that for a taxi.

Kammerman's Atlantic City Marina is on the other side of Clam Creek Basin from the state marina. It offers slips for transients to 75 feet, showers, a marine supply store, fuel, mechanics' services, and free transportation to anywhere in Atlantic City. They monitor Ch-16.

Harrah's Marina is located just west of the Brigantine Bridge. The dock master can be reached on VHF Ch-9 or Ch-16. Entrance into, and exit from, the slips can be tricky when the tide flow is at its peak. The full-service, 70-slip marina charges $1.10/foot/day for slips, which includes water, showers, and laundry. Cable-TV and shore power are also at dockside. From the slip, the skipper can even order a meal, which is delivered directly to the boat.

The boardwalk, the first in the world, was built in 1870, and now extends four miles along the ocean south of Atlantic City's inlet, Absecon Inlet. All along

A view of the Sen. Frank S. Farley State Marina at night

the boardwalk are small shops, amusements, food vendors and, of course, salt-water taffy. There are several piers jutting out into the Atlantic along the city's oceanfront. The Steel Pier, in front of the Taj Mahal Casino, is an amusement pier; while Ocean One Pier, at the end of Arkansas Avenue and just north of the Convention Center, is a mall, with stores, snack bars, and restaurants.

Casinos, both along the boardwalk and near the marinas, offer gambling, shops, and restaurants, along with big-name shows that rival those of Las Vegas. A visit to Atlantic City now is a far cry from my first visit there in the early thirties, when I was seven years old. Then, my brother and I were not allowed on the beach because our bathing suits didn't have tops.

In Atlantic City there are transportation connections by car, bus, rail (on Amtrak), or plane (to and from Atlantic City International Airport or Bader Field Airport, the municipal airport next to the ICW). By land it is about one hour to Philadelphia, two and a half hours to New York City and four hours to Washington, D.C. Although it is hard to conceive, nearly one-third of the population of the United States lives within 300 miles of Atlantic City.

The first Atlantic City entrepreneurs paid four cents an acre for the property where the city stands now. This was a bargain compared to the twenty-four cents an acre paid for property on the mainland. Now, that same twenty-four cents can't even buy one pull on the slot machine.

Chart 5.3 Atlantic City (reproduced from NOAA's Chart #12316)

After the poorer and wiser crew has had their obligatory try at breaking the bank, we are ready to resume our cruise.

Heading south from Atlantic City, we have two options—or we may have one, depending on the boat. Boats with drafts of over 4 feet can expect to touch bottom more than once on the shallow ICW between Atlantic City and Cape May. With enough power they may be able to push themselves through the muddy bottom. Boats with masts of over thirty-five feet will be unable to make the inland trip at all, due to several 35-foot fixed bridges across the Intracoastal Waterway. In boats restricted by draft or mast height, the trip south will have to be made in the ocean, by going out the Absecon Inlet and down along the shore to the Cape May Inlet, formerly known as Cold Spring Harbor Inlet.

Atlantic City's inlet is wide, deep, and easy to use. The only warning here is to avoid the shoal area that extends well out into the ocean from the north jetty.

The Intracoastal Waterway route to Cape May is covered in the next chapter, and the offshore passage, the ocean trip to Cape May, is described in chapter 7.

Chapter Six

The Intracoastal Waterway from Atlantic City to Cape May and Cape May Ashore

*J*ust inside Atlantic City's Absecon Inlet, to the west of the highway bridge at ICW mile 65, the Intracoastal Waterway continues south past Atlantic City. The ICW between here and Cape May is crossed by several fixed bridges with 35-foot clearances, limiting the waterway to all but the smallest of sailboats. There are also numerous bascule bridges, both road and rail, with restricted openings during the summer months. To make things worse, water depth in several spots has shoaled to less than four feet. It is no wonder that skippers of most medium- to large-sized powerboats and skippers of nearly all sailboats do not consider this section of the Intracoastal Waterway as a viable route south from Atlantic City.

The ocean trip to Cape May from Atlantic City is 40 miles long. Inlets between Atlantic City and Cape May are marginal in good weather and shouldn't even be considered as a refuge during stormy conditions. Once outside, we're committed to Cape May Inlet or to a return to Atlantic City's Inlet, Absecon Inlet. When fog, high winds, or the threat of a storm is in the forecast and the safety of a trip down the coast is in doubt, the restrictions of the optional inside passage should be reconsidered. Boats with a draft of over three feet must remember that the nominal depths of the inside passage can be influenced considerably by blow-in and blow-out tides. After a prolonged west wind, the ICW will be shallower than normal, as much as a foot or more; whereas, an east or northeast wind will provide a bonus in water depth but not in bridge clearance. If the weather is kicking up, skippers of boats precluded from the inside passage by the ICW's limitations might well consider a day of boat-keeping, another try at the casinos, a walk on the boardwalk, or a day on the beach. When planning

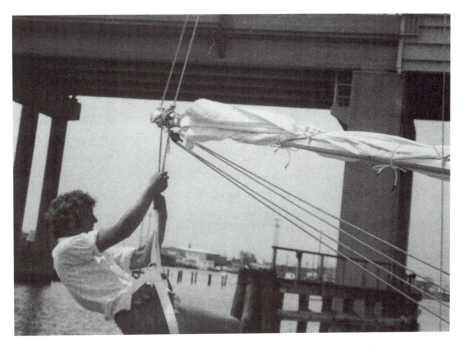

Negotiating the fixed bridges, with Tom out on the end of the boom

any coastal or intracoastal cruise, it is wise to include a few buffer days for just such weather-related delays.

When using the ICW heading south, the first bridge one encounters is the bascule bridge (20-foot closed clearance) at Absecon Boulevard. The first of the 35-foot fixed bridges, a little farther south, is at ICW mile 69, and a railroad bridge with 20-foot clearance is just to its north. The railroad bridge is scheduled to open between twenty and thirty minutes after the hour, between 6 A.M. and 11 P.M., but this isn't always the case. Don't anchor in this area while waiting; there are underwater cables, and the warning on the chart can be easily overlooked.

Continuing south along the inner side of Atlantic City, one will find facilities for transients, with a few slips for transients and a fuel dock just to the south of the Albany Avenue bascule bridge (mile 70). This bascule bridge has a 10-foot closed clearance and opens on the hour and half-hour between 9 A.M. and 9 P.M., June 1 through September 30, although sometimes an opening will be skipped if the 4 P.M. to 6 P.M. highway traffic is too congested.

The Dorset Avenue bridge at Ventnor Heights has a closed 9-foot clearance, and scheduled opening times are fifteen and forty-five minutes past the hour, between 9:15 A.M. and 9:15 P.M., from June 1 to September 30. The nonuniformity of opening hours for the bridges on the ICW between Atlantic City and Cape

May was planned. It was determined that this would allow ICW traffic to progress from one bridge to another with little delay if it traveled at a no-wake speed. Unfortunately, it seldom works this way.

Farther south, on Absecon Island, we pass Ventnor and then Margate, reaching the end of the monopoly-board names. Ventnor and Margate have managed to remain relatively low-key in their principal function as suburbs of Atlantic City, and our trip along the waterway takes on a more residential flavor.

At ICW mile 74 the bascule bridge has a closed clearance of 14 feet, and just to its south, in Margate, there are several small-craft facilities. Just before reaching Ocean City one passes under a bascule bridge at mile 78 that has a 9-foot closed clearance. In 1986 a fixed bridge with a 53-foot clearance (intended to replace the bascule bridge) was begun, but at this writing it has not yet been completed.

There are several very large marinas off the ICW at Ocean City, and they welcome transients. Harbor House Marina monitors Ch-16; it has slips, showers, washers and dryers, a pool, a restaurant, a hotel, fuel, and repair facilities. It is located south of Ocean City's Great Egg Harbor Inlet, about a mile below the bascule bridge, and south of the Coast Guard station. The huge Seaview Harbor Marina and Islander Restaurant, with slips for transients, fuel, pool, showers, car rental service, pump-out, and repair facilities, is just to the north of the inlet, before the fixed bridge. It monitors both Ch-10 and Ch-16. Other marinas are scattered along Ocean City's inland waterfront.

Ocean City caters to families, especially to toddlers. The Wonderland Pier at 6th Street and Playland at 10th Street provide fun for kids and, of course, there is always Ocean City's clean ocean beach. In the summertime Ocean City's population soars to more than 125,000. To get away from the crowds, try Corsons Inlet State Park at the tip of the island.

The Ocean City Coast Guard station cannot be seen from the ICW, except for its tall flagpole. The station itself is tucked into a sort of cul-de-sac off the main channel.

When listening to the weather channels on the VHF-FM Marine Band, one will frequently hear forecasts given for Ocean City. These forecasts refer to Ocean City, Maryland, which is located on one of the barrier islands of the Delmarva, 42 miles south of Cape May. Since this part of Maryland is included in the local weather forecasts, don't be misled into thinking that the reference is to Ocean City, New Jersey.

New Jersey's Ocean City was established as a dry town by the three Lake brothers, all Methodist ministers, who purchased the land in 1879, and some of their original restrictions on liquors are still written into the deeds today.

In present-day Ocean City, New Jersey, there are several residential marinas, that is, co-ops or condos with boat slips included. For several years now, marina owners have found it more profitable to close down their marina operations and to build complexes of this type; the trend is seen throughout the nation's waterways. Many times, when looking for a once-visited boatyard, we've discovered that it's been replaced by one of these nonpublic facilities.

Just south of Great Egg Harbor Inlet, at Ocean City, a marked waterway branches off the ICW heading west to Somers Point, less than two miles away, where there are small-craft facilities with fuel, marine repairs, haul-out, shops, and restaurants along the waterfront. Just beyond Somers Point, on the west end of Great Egg Harbor, Tuckahoe River and Great Egg Harbor River provide interesting side trips. Both of these deep rivers wend their way through wetlands into unspoiled pine barrens. The Great Egg Harbor River is navigable for 13 miles, to Mays Landing, and the Tuckahoe River for 7 miles, to Tuckahoe. One can also explore Patcong Creek, Cedar Swamp Creek, Middle River, or Powell Creek, all on the western end of Great Egg Harbor.

As we return to the ICW after our explorations of the little streams to the west, we encounter a bascule bridge across the waterway at Ocean City that has a closed clearance of 14 feet and will open on demand, except on weekends and holidays between Memorial Day and Labor Day, from 11 A.M. to 5 P.M. During these times, openings are restricted to the hour and the half-hour.

A 35-foot fixed bridge on the ICW at mile 84.3 prevents large sailboats, that have entered Great Egg Harbor Inlet at Ocean City, from continuing further south. Just north of this bridge, on the west side of the ICW, is a full-service marina with berths for transients, fuel, and repair facilities. About two miles to the south of this 35-foot fixed bridge, at mile 86.6, the railroad swing bridge shown on the chart was being demolished and may now be gone.

Several years ago my wife Elsie and I, along with our son Tom, were bringing a small sailboat up from the Florida Keys to New Jersey. It was the spring of the year and the ocean was still acting temperamentally. At Cape May, the offshore trip looked marginal for the type of craft we were sailing, and its total height was just over 37 feet, so we elected to try the inside passage through the several 35-foot fixed bridges.

As we approached the first fixed bridge, the clearance marker along the bridge abutment showed 35.5 feet; we needed to reduce our height by a foot and a half. Tom fastened himself to the end of the boom in a bosun's chair, and we swung him out over the water. Then, with both Elsie and I hanging over on the same side, we were able to heel the boat over just enough to make it through. We performed the same maneuver at each of the 35-foot fixed bridges, until finally arriving at Atlantic City. I'm sure we presented an entertaining diversion for the people on shore.

Continuing south, the ICW now picks its way through sedges and marsh-lands to the west of Corsons Inlet. At ICW pole number 328 a marked waterway heads off to the east. Following this side channel to Strathmere on the barrier island a mile and a half away, we find several marinas with fuel, marina sup-plies, and repair facilities.

At Sea Isle City, on the same island, a 35-foot fixed bridge at Mile 93.6, connects the island to the mainland. A railroad line reached Sea Isle City in 1884, and it burgeoned as a mecca for Philadelphia vacationers. At that time, the tracks were built through Sea Isle City to Townsends Inlet at the south of the island and, in 1889, two railroad drawbridges were constructed across Town-sends Inlet, leading to the city of Avalon on Seven Mile Beach.

In the last few years Sea Isle City has become popular with the younger crowd, teen-agers and adults between the ages of twenty and thirty. The area also boasts a large commercial fishing industry, which is reflected in the nu-merous seafood restaurants and fish markets on shore.

Just off the ICW, at Avalon, there are three channels that head east off the waterway: Cornell Harbor, Pennsylvania Harbor, and Princeton Harbor. Al-though the ends of these harbors are connected by water along Avalon's water-front, they are separated by fixed bridges with just a few feet of clearance, preventing their use by anything but very small boats. One of the several marinas at Avalon is the Commodore Bay Marina, located just south of the Townsends Inlet bridge, at the end of Cornell Harbor. It monitors Ch-16 and welcomes transients. The Avalon Pointe Marina is located a little farther south, on the west bank of the ICW. It offers a full line of services, welcomes tran-sients, and also monitors Ch-16.

As the ICW progresses south, inside of Seven Mile Island from Avalon, an-other 35-foot fixed bridge is encountered, the last fixed bridge before Cape May.

At this point, the ICW passes close to the town of Stone Harbor, where residential homes dominate the waterfront. On the northwest side of the bascule bridge at Stone Harbor one will find the Stone Harbor Marina. The ICW bridge next to the marina, with a 10-foot closed clearance, has restricted open-ing hours on weekends and holidays, between Memorial Day and Labor Day. It will open for boat traffic on the hour and every twenty minutes thereafter, be-tween 6 A.M. and 6 P.M.

About half a mile down the road, to the west of the marina and the bascule bridge (and, appropriately, in the wetlands), travelers will discover the attrac-tive cedar-shake building housing the Wetlands Institute. The institute offers educational programs and a coastal museum, with exhibits for young and old. The institute is a private, nonprofit organization supported by gifts and dona-

The Wetlands Institute at Stone Harbor

tions. Its calendar of both indoor and outdoor programs provides diversions and education for every one, from the toddler to the serious adult environmentalist. The lobby of the institute houses a gift shop as well as a book store with a huge variety of books on wildlife and ecology.

South of Stone Harbor, there is a bascule bridge that carries mainland traffic to North Wildwood. To eliminate the long weekend delays for both boaters and motorists, this bascule bridge (with 8-foot closed clearance) at mile 105.2 is being replaced by a high arching fixed bridge with 55 feet of clearance. When the new bridge is completed, the bascule bridge will be removed.

The railroad bridge shown on the chart at mile 107.5 no longer exists, and before removal its western pier collapsed into the waterway. It's a good idea to give this side of the channel a wide berth.

The waterway now passes Wildwood and Wildwood Crest. Sunset Lake is a comparatively deep harbor next to Wildwood Crest, and either of the two charted entrances can be used.

Through the years the character of the Wildwoods has changed markedly, from a wooded barrier island of little economic value to the bustling, popular ocean-side resort of today. The land now called Wildwood and Wildwood Crest was sold by its owner, in 1700 or thereabout, for nine pounds; he used the money to buy a calico dress for his wife.

Almost two centuries later, in 1890, Philip Baker, a state senator from Cumberland County, purchased one hundred acres. At that time the property was a thick forest of oaks and cedars, with wild grapevines climbing to the treetops. Beneath the canopy, moss and wildflowers hung from the branches, and huge huckleberry bushes grew on the forest floor. It was truly a wild wood; Wildwood was an appropriate name. This didn't last long, however.

In 1912 an automobile bridge was built across the wetlands to Wildwood, and a boardwalk was constructed, making Wildwood into an amusement center. Property was parceled off and Wildwood, along with the wild woods, had the dubitable distinction of being propelled into the twentieth century. Today, the boardwalk along Wildwood's wide beaches is an attraction for those seeking rides, fast food, t-shirt shops, and an amusement-park atmosphere.

At Wildwood Crest, just north of the Cape May Inlet and Cape May Harbor, one will find the Two Mile Landing Marina. It monitors Ch-16 and has slips for transient boats that are up to one hundred feet long, with good approach and dockside depth, along with two restaurants. Skippers of large powerboats, or of sailboats that are unable to use the ICW south of Atlantic City, can reach the marina by going a short way north from Cape May Harbor or Cape May Inlet. The marina can easily be seen off the ICW to the east after passing through the bascule bridge at the north end of Cape May Harbor. Whenever marinas in Cape May Harbor are booked solid, and hanging on the hook is not appealing, this marina, which is off the beaten track, is worth investigating. For those who would like to anchor out, the deep waterway between the ICW and the Two Mile Landing Marina is a quiet and protected location. From here it is not too far to take a dinghy with an outboard into Cape May for supplies.

A few miles farther south the waterway passes inside of the Cape May Inlet, entering Cape May Harbor and marking the southern end of the New Jersey Intracoastal Waterway (chart 6.1). The best is saved until the last.

The harbor at Cape May is a cozy one, completely protected from storms. There are three narrow entrances to the harbor: the ICW to the north, the Cape May Inlet to the east (which is one of the best on the New Jersey coast), and the Cape May Canal leading to Delaware Bay on the west. The harbor is a popular layover spot for boats waiting out good weather before heading in one of three directions: west across Delaware Bay, north up the Atlantic coast to Atlantic City or beyond, or south on the ocean side of the Delmarva, toward Chesapeake Bay. A layover here is a good excuse, if one is needed, to enjoy the pleasures of this southern tip of New Jersey, which few realize is south of Baltimore, Maryland.

It is a good idea to make reservations at one of the numerous marinas or yacht clubs here; when fishing tournaments are held offshore, slips for tran-

The Coast Guard station in Cape May Harbor

Cape May Harbor

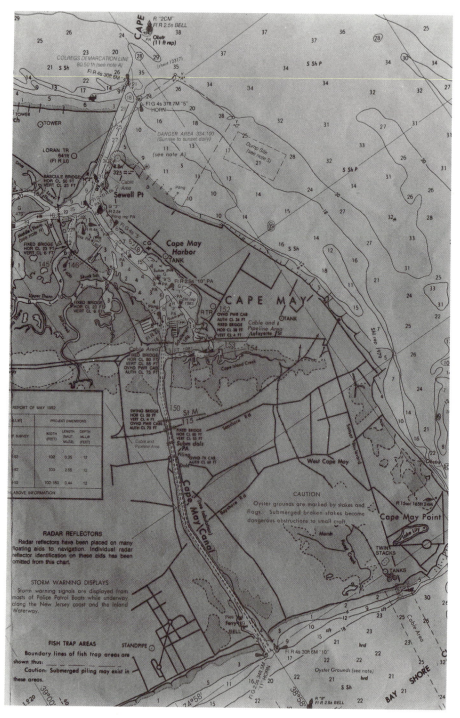

Chart 6.1 Cape May (reproduced from NOAA's Chart #12304)

sients don't exist. It is possible, though, to anchor well off the channel in the harbor and take the dink in to shore, where most of the places of interest are within walking or biking distance. Due to its flat terrain, Cape May is an ideal walking or biking area, and if there are no bikes on board, they can be rented at several locations on shore.

The town of Cape May, with its Victorian architecture and meticulously kept homes, has been declared a national historic landmark. Much of the town has changed little since the end of the last century. It is hard not to fall in love with Cape May, and a tour makes a fascinating excursion. The oceanfront is two miles away from the harbor, and an outdoor pedestrian mall is somewhat closer. The immense sea wall along Cape May's waterfront was built after the devastating nor'easter in the spring of 1962, which wreaked havoc all along the New Jersey coast and flooded most of the city.

One will find that many of the old Victorian homes in town, especially those along the oceanfront, have been turned into bed-and-breakfast hotels, where reservations are required during the summer season.

Cape May is proud of its history, and the past still pleasantly flavors the town's ambiance. In a time when new, modern accommodations are venerated and the word old is usually meant as a condemnation, it is refreshing to visit Cape May.

Going back in time, the first permanent European settlers at the cape were New England whalers, who arrived in the mid-1600s. Travelers from Philadelphia were the first to use Cape May as a vacation resort, arriving by steamboat and sailing packet from the Delaware River and Delaware Bay in the early 1800s. Access to Cape May in those days was primarily by boat, since the roads to the cape remained wretched. A railroad finally terminated there in 1863, adding impetus to recreational development.

When the Garden State Parkway arrived at Cape May in 1954, it was feared the town would succumb to glitter and glitz, which usually results from easy access. Fortunately, it has remained essentially quaint, and the glitter and glitz seekers must find it elsewhere.

If the opportunity exists, we never miss the Cape May Point State Park, 4 miles from the harbor (taking Sunset Boulevard west, then Lighthouse Road off to the left). Cape May Point Park is one of the most popular bird-watching sites in North America. It is on the Atlantic flyway, the natural route of migrating birds that head north or south in the spring and fall, and it is also a wetland area that provides refuge to flocks awaiting good weather for the Delaware Bay crossing or for resting after the crossing. During the spring and autumn migrations more than 360 species have been counted, and it is common both at the point and in Cape May proper to see field glasses aplenty. Guided bird walks

The Victorian homes of Cape May

are given at the park; bird-watching platforms have been erected; and there is a nature museum close to the lighthouse. The park offers three miles of trails and boardwalks, and self-guided nature trail information is available at the park office. Surf fishing is permitted, and picnic sites with tables and grills are provided.

For those who are interested, just beyond the breakers, off the ocean beach at the park, one will find a World War II concrete artillery bunker that, when built in 1942, was located on a high sand dune 900 feet inland. The bunker's armament consisted of four 155mm coast artillery guns and some six-inch guns. Its walls and roof are made of six-foot-thick reinforced concrete. A sister bunker, built to guard the cape at the southern entrance to Delaware Bay, stands firm at Cape Henlopen near Lewes, Delaware.

The old trolley tracks that went south from the town of Cape May and were in use from 1892 to 1918 are now at the bottom of the ocean about a quarter-mile offshore. Both tracks and bunker provide a dramatic example of the changeable nature of the shoreline along this southern tip of New Jersey.

This rapidly changing shoreline has taken its toll on lighthouses at the cape. Its first lighthouse was built in 1823, but soon the sea encroached on its base; it was undermined and collapsed. The second one, built in 1847 about 600 yards from the present lighthouse, suffered the same fate. The lighthouse that now

The World War II artillery bunker off Cape May Point

stands at the park was erected in 1859. It is 170 feet high, with walls eight feet thick at the base and, for the foreseeable future, it seems to be safe. The lighthouse is open to the public ($3.50 for adults and $1.00 for children). It is a climb of 199 steps to the top, where a spectacular view of New Jersey's southern cape awaits. The lighthouse is only one of two along the New Jersey coastline that are still navigational, the other being the Sandy Hook Lighthouse.

At the end of Sunset Boulevard, the Delaware Bay Beach called Sunset Beach is located. Near the beach are the remains of the freighter *Atlantus,* which was built of concrete (due to the steel shortage during World War I) by the Liberty Shipbuilding Company in Wilmington, Delaware. From this bay beach one can see the major shipping on Delaware Bay's main channel and the ferries going back and forth between Cape May and Lewes (pronounced "Lewis"), Delaware. On a clear day, when standing on a sand dune, one can see the low coastline of Cape Henlopen, Delaware, to the south. Since this beach is on the bay, waters are calmer and safer and can be enjoyed by small children.

On all of Cape May's beaches one can have fun looking for the so-called Cape May diamonds. These small quartz, semiprecious stones come in all sizes, and many of Cape May's stores sell them polished and cut or mounted in jewelry.

Some other points of interest near the town include the Coast Guard's basic-training center (the only one in the country); The Cape May Historical Museum, at the Cape May Court House on Route 9; and a 128-acre zoo at Cape May County Park, about ten miles north of town.

There are several restaurants close to the harbor and many more near the center of town, and the Wawa store near the harbor will deliver package meals and other items directly to your boat. A particular favorite of boaters is The Lobster House, located next to the commercial fishing docks at the southwest end of the harbor. It is a restaurant we always visit during one of our cruises. It has an outdoor raw-fish bar, a large inside dining room overlooking the water, a seafood store with an unbelievable selection, and a cocktail bar aboard the vintage Grand Banks schooner *American* (no relation to the schooner *America* of America's Cup fame), which is at dockside next to the restaurant. The restaurant's decor includes model ships, half-hulls, old photographs, and newspaper articles that recall the area's fishing heritage.

The property adjoining the Lobster House is occupied by Utsch's Marina, a family-owned-and-operated business. It has slips for transients, fuel, a large marine store, showers, a travel-lift, and it can handle hull and engine repairs. The marina entrance can be reached by turning 90° at ICW flashing-red number 14, and then proceeding about twenty feet off the marina's bulkhead to the entrance. Alternately, it can be entered by heading south off the ICW toward the

Utsch's Marina in Cape May Harbor, next to the Cape May Canal

The Cape May Canal

fishing docks at flashing-red number 10, passing between buoys numbered 1 and 2, and proceeding to the marina entrance. This latter approach should only be used by skippers of shoal-draft craft at low tide. Skippers of deep-draft boats should check with the marina for approach depths if there is any question. The marina monitors Ch-16. Utsch's Marina is representative of the several fine marinas at the southwestern end of Cape May Harbor.

When it's finally time to say a reluctant farewell to Cape May Harbor and to continue on our cruise, several options present themselves. At the northeastern corner of Cape May Harbor, we can take the Intracoastal Waterway—the inland route we described earlier in the chapter. Also at the northeastern corner of the harbor is Cape May Inlet, which is our access to the ocean and an ocean trip north toward Atlantic City, Sandy Hook, and New York Harbor, or south to the ocean entrance of Delaware Bay. The more venturesome can use the Cape May Inlet as a jumping-off point for an ocean trip outside the Delmarva Peninsula, to the Chesapeake or beyond, or even as a rhumb line to the eastern tip of Long Island and on to New England waters.

At the southwestern corner of Cape May Harbor is the entrance to the Cape May Canal, which joins Cape May Harbor with Delaware Bay—the bay being on the western shore of the Cape May peninsula (chart 6.2). There are several

*C*hart 6.2 Cape May Harbor (reproduced from NOAA's Chart #12317)

opportunities for gunkholing the small streams off Delaware Bay, or one can travel to the Chesapeake and Delaware Canal, which leads to the north end of Chesapeake Bay. One can also go past the Chesapeake and Dealware Canal and follow the Delaware River up to its head of navigation at Trenton.

In the next chapter we will look at the alternate way of reaching Cape May, the offshore passage. Then, in the following chapter, chapter 8, we'll explore Delaware Bay and its tributaries.

Chapter Seven

The Offshore Passage: Manasquan Inlet to Cape May

*T*he previous four chapters have dealt with the inside passage, New Jersey's Intracoastal Waterway from Manasquan to Cape May. Some boat owners, under the constraints of very high masts, deep keels, or time, will be unable or unwilling to take this leisurely shoal-draft route south. For them, the offshore route along the New Jersey coast is the alternative.

In chapter 3, I discussed the offshore trip from Sandy Hook down the coast to Manasquan Inlet and through the inlet into the Intracoastal Waterway. Now, let's take a look at the ocean-going trip from Manasquan Inlet south to Cape May.

The distance by ocean from Manasquan Inlet to the Cape May Inlet is 85 nautical miles (98 statute miles). For a boat leaving from Sandy Hook and taking the ocean route to Cape May, the total distance is 127 statute miles. It is obvious that displacement hulls, such as most sailboats and trawler-type powerboats have, will be unable to complete this trip down the coast of New Jersey during daylight hours, even under ideal conditions. If a nighttime stopover on inland waters, using one of the inlets, is not planned, a crew competent in night passages and able to stand watches will be necessary.

It should be remembered that electing to take the ocean route doesn't limit one's options; a combination of offshore and inland passages can be combined, depending on weather and personal interests.

Those traveling in high-speed powerboats will have to calculate the time it will take for the offshore trip according to the expected boat speed; but, remember that this boat speed could be severely compromised by wave conditions. One advantage to traveling in a high-speed powerboat and using the ocean route is that speed is not restricted by numerous no-wake zones, as it is on the

⚓ ⚓

ICW. For the sailor, there is a greater opportunity to hoist sail on the offshore passage, and the constant changes in sail trim and the delays for bridges that one encounters on the ICW is eliminated. Another advantage to the offshore route is that the nearly straight-line passage is about fifteen miles shorter than is the passage along the ICW route between Manasquan and Cape May. In a displacement-hull craft this can easily save travelers two hours or more.

A disadvantage to this route is that one must factor into the equation the possibility of changing weather conditions. If the weather starts kicking up, is the boat seaworthy enough to continue the passage safely? Will its draft restrictions make it unable to enter one of the inlets? Will there be a safe inlet nearby if weather conditions deteriorate? These are important considerations since, when the weather gets rough, many of New Jersey's inlets become dangerous and cannot be used. Do we know the boat well enough and how it will handle in rough seas? Is the engine in good shape, and is there enough fuel for the planned passage? We must always keep in mind that the ocean, like a mischievous child, doesn't like to obey the rules and frequently does the unexpected. It doesn't hurt to look at weather forecasts with a jaundiced eye.

Storms and shipwrecks along the New Jersey coast have been a fact of life since the days of Henry Hudson's explorations. No one knows how many ships have been violently delivered onto the beaches of New Jersey, but the estimates are several thousand, probably one for every few hundred yards along our shoreline. In one stormy month, during the winter of 1826/27, more than two hundred ships were wrecked on these shores. These wrecks provided unexpected bounty for the poor fishing families that lived along the coast, and there is even some evidence that ships were enticed ashore with false signals sent by the so-called wreckers or mooncussers on land.

From the standpoint of the onshore salvager, one of the more memorable shipwrecks occurred in the spring of 1897. The two-masted sailing ship *Francis,* having sailed out of California with a full cargo, was being driven ashore on Long Beach Island. Seeing that the ship's destruction was near, the island residents launched their surf boats and rescued all twenty-five persons on board just before the *Francis* was grounded in the surf line and began breaking up. When the cargo started drifting to shore, word spread throughout the island, and every resident headed for the beach. Some crates that drifted ashore contained food, but the major part of the cargo consisted of barrels of California wine, port, and sherry, and crates of bottled champagne, madeira, and brandy. A beach party ensued that lasted two days—it was truly a tight little island. By the morning of the third day an island-wide epidemic of hangover existed, and things quieted down considerably. The cargo was listed as lost at sea.

During both world wars, it wasn't only the weather but German U-Boats that sent ships to the bottom along our coast. Older shore residents remember the many nights that tankers and freighters could be seen burning offshore. For years, the high water mark on the beaches was edged with black oil.

Three of the worst storms to visit the New Jersey coast in this century were the 1944 hurricane, the 1962 spring nor'easter, and the nor'easter of December 1992. In each of these storms wind-blown waves washed across the barrier islands, and the inland bays rose to unprecedented heights. Although hurricanes are what everyone dreads, it is frequently the prolonged nor'easters that do the most damage along this coastline.

Now, let's leave this talk of storms and shipwrecks and take a calmer look at the offshore trip from Manasquan south to Cape May.

The principal improved inlets along the New Jersey coast, that is, those with breakwaters and dredging programs are: Shark River, Manasquan, Barnegat, Absecon (Atlantic City), and Cape May (formerly Cold Spring Harbor Inlet). The other, unimproved inlets are best used while employing local knowledge and extreme caution, or not at all. These inlets are not for the marginally experienced.

The coast along this part of the New Jersey shore stretches south-southwest in a nearly straight line from Manasquan to the next inlet, Barnegat Inlet, 25 miles to the south. Nearly all inlets along the New Jersey coast are characterized by shoals near the mouth of the inlet that extend well offshore. Over the last few centuries these shoals have accounted for innumerable shipwrecks. Frequently, when time is not a constraint, we enjoy traveling along the coast, close to shore. It enables us to see the sights and can give protection from the winds and waves if the wind is coming from onshore. But, I always remember, when approaching inlets, to check the chart and to move out well beyond the shoals. When time is of the essence or when we are traveling in fog, we stay well offshore on rhumb-line courses that provide the shortest route and keep us well to seaward of the inlet shoals. An example of this would be the trip between Atlantic City and the sea buoy off Wildwood, which is considerably shorter and safer than is following the coast.

Wind conditions should be seriously considered when electing to begin the offshore passage along New Jersey's coast. When the wind is from the west, even if very strong, the waves in the ocean close to the coast are small. Strong winds from the northeast, east, or southeast are another matter and should be evaluated before one commits to the offshore passage. Since wave heights are proportional to the wind speed and the *fetch* of these winds, that is, the distance the wind has had to form them, a prolonged wind blowing in from the ocean can make things a bit lumpy.

One of the most positive things we've noticed during our trips in the last few years is the dramatic increase in water quality as we cruise along the shore-line. Last year, when we looked down into the water near shore, we were reminded of being in the Caribbean, and each year we encounter more schools of dolphins and whales traveling along the coast.

As we begin our offshore passage south from Manasquan, the Ferris wheel and roller-coaster will be the first distinctive landmarks that identify Seaside Heights. Just below Seaside, development on shore ends as we come abreast of Island Beach State Park. On a clear day we'll be able to see the red top of Barnegat Lighthouse to the south, raising its head above the sand dunes of Island Beach and providing an unmistakable fix.

Barnegat Lighthouse, 161 feet high, red on its upper half and white on its lower half, is listed on the charts as abandoned. It is no longer navigational, and only shows a token light. For purposes of coastal navigation at night, the location of Barnegat Inlet is easily seen by the demarcation line between the dark shores of Island Beach State Park and the lights of Long Beach Island, making the lighthouse superfluous. Barnegat Inlet is protected by jetties on the north and south. The jetties have towers at their outer ends, and there's a fog signal on the south jetty. There is a Coast Guard station near the lighthouse, in the town of Barnegat Light. It can be reached on VHF Ch-16 or Ch-22A.

Barnegat Inlet should *only* be used under ideal sea conditions, preferably on a rising tide and, if possible, while watching and following one of the local commercial fishing boats into the entrance channel. This is a prudent approach, since the location of the entrance bars and of deep water changes with every storm. As with all New Jersey inlets, tides sweep in and out from the Atlantic Ocean with two high and two low every day, so that the bottom contours as well as the shoreline is in a constant state of change. One should be aware when approaching Barnegat Inlet that the northern breakwater is submerged at high tide and will not show up on radar. Taking a shortcut between the outer tower and the shore means going on the rocks. When there are breakers across the entrance bar, the rule is: don't use the inlet; at the very least, a call to the Coast Guard is recommended. Whenever I use Barnegat Inlet, even though I've used it all my life, everyone aboard dons life jackets—it's a given. Several people die here nearly every year.

The name Barnegat is a corruption of the original Dutch description "Barende-gat," or "Breakers Inlet," and it is appropriately named, since breakers across the entrance can occur even on relatively calm days. As with most inlets, going out is always easier than is returning. Once, when going out, I powered into the curl of a huge breaker, which broke on the foredeck and cabin top, soaking me from head to foot and nearly filling the cockpit. Another time I received a real scare. As I was entering the inlet, the wave I was riding began to

Aerial view of Barnegat Inlet. To the north of the inlet is the undeveloped Island Beach State Park, and to the south the resort island of Long Beach Island. Note the change of direction of the shoreline at Barnegat Inlet and the typical shoals that extend well offshore (photo courtesy of Keith Hamilton, Studio-9, Waretown).

break, and I surfed all the way through the inlet at high speed on the face of the breaker between the stone jetties. I repeated to myself, "Don't broach! Don't broach!" all the way in.

In 1991 a multimillion dollar south jetty project was completed in the hope of deepening and stabilizing Barnegat Inlet. Although it has seemed to help, it is too soon to tell whether the anticipated results will materialize. One thing that is certain is that tidal currents within the inlet have increased considerably, and at the height of the tide change underpowered auxiliaries will have a hard time bucking an opposing current. This increased tidal flow, caused by the recent dredging, may have been an important contributing factor in the Barnegat Bay flood tides of Halloween 1991 and in the December nor'easter of 1992.

As we pass Barnegat Inlet, the coastline takes a turn to the southwest and continues in that direction all the way to Cape May (chart 7.1). Sailors who have

Chart 7.1 Barnegat Inlet (reproduced from NOAA's Chart #12324)

been close-hauled to the prevailing southwest winds up to now may find they have to fire up the iron wind or else tack down the coast.

The next inlet south of Barnegat is 22 miles away, at the end of Long Beach Island.

This island was the site of an unusual encounter during the War of 1812. The USS *Constitution* (*Old Ironsides,* which is now berthed in Boston Harbor) was sailing up the New Jersey coast from the Chesapeake, destined for New York Harbor. At twilight on July 17, 1813, in the failing light, Captain Isaac Hull sighted sails and believed them to be the American ships with whom he had a rendezvous. The wind was dying, and he dropped anchor near the south end of Long Beach Island so that the *Constitution* would not drift ashore.

At first light the next morning, with the fog beginning to lift, Hull discovered he was anchored near a British flotilla that consisted of five ships carrying 172 cannon. He had no U.S. flag flying, so he decided to steal away in spite of the glassy, calm sea surface and the absense of wind; he launched the ship's boats, silently raised anchor, and towed the *Constitution* away from the British fleet.

It wasn't long before the British discovered what was happening and opened up with broadsides from all five ships' guns, but by now the *Constitution* was out of range. Captain Hull ordered the American flag hoisted and returned fire from his stern canons, and although he too was out of range, the cannonade helped propel the ship forward.

Then, in an effort to put even more room between themselves and the British, the American crew began kedging, by rowing small anchors out ahead in the longboats and hauling up to them from the deck of the ship. Soon the British began doing the same. This labor continued on the unusually still sea for three days. The *Constitution* and the British flotilla pulled themselves up the coast, past Barnegat Inlet and Island Beach until a squall allowed the *Constitution* to hoist sail and escape.

As we make our way south, along the tortuous route taken by the *Constitution,* we near the southern end of Long Beach Island; the last two miles at the south end of the island are undeveloped and have been set aside as a wildlife refuge.

Just beyond the refuge are the twin inlets of Beach Haven and Little Egg. Because of the numerous wrecks and shoals, and the changing channel, Beach Haven Inlet on the north has been officially closed to navigation by the Coast Guard; the inlet is unmarked. It appears that it is on its way to becoming dry land and a part of Long Beach Island. If one has to use an inlet in this area, Little Egg Inlet is the only viable one, close to the south of the old Beach Haven Inlet. It is well buoyed, but these are uncharted due to the constantly shifting shoals. The buoys marking the inlet are center-channel buoys (vertical red and white

Aerial view of the sourthern tip of Long Beach Island and the twin inlets of Beach Haven and Little Egg (photo courtesy of Keith Hamilton, Studio-9, Waretown)

stripes) with sequential letters that start with A at the seaward end of this two-mile-long channel. Keep a sharp eye out for dog-leg turns, which can easily be overlooked.

In heavy weather Little Egg Inlet should also be avoided by the inexperienced, since breakers can form all the way across the bar and are frequently on the beam.

Two and a half miles down the coast from Little Egg Inlet is Brigantine Inlet, which has shoaled-in to such an extent that even the smallest of boats with local knowledge consider it unsafe. Cross this one off your list.

Nearly ten miles below the twin inlets of Beach Haven and Little Egg is Absecon Inlet, one of the best on the coast. The high rises and casinos make it obvious that this is Atlantic City, which is on Absecon Island. It is home to a large fleet of commercial fishing boats as well as to recreational craft. The inlet is frequently used by transients who have spent one or more days sightseeing and who will be making the offshore trip north to New York Harbor or south to Delaware Bay.

Aerial view of Atlantic City. Note the large expanses of wetlands to the west of the city through which the ICW meanders (photo courtesy of Keith Hamilton, Studio-9, Waretown).

The great granite rocks of the north and south jetties are far apart, making this inlet the broadest of New Jersey's improved inlets. Don't come in too close to shore when approaching from the north; a shoal extends well to seaward of the north jetty and has been responsible for many wrecks.

When a break in the offshore passage from Manasquan to Cape May is planned, or if the weather is becoming marginal and the seas are beginning to kick up, the Absecon Inlet at Atlantic City is the inlet to use for an overnight berth, a refuge, a chance for a meal ashore, some sightseeing, or a try at the gambling tables. (For more information on Atlantic City marinas and facilities, see chapter 5.)

The 167-foot tall Absecon Lighthouse at Atlantic City, like Barnegat Lighthouse, is now listed as abandoned and is even difficult to locate from offshore, having been obscured by the surrounding high rises and casinos. When it was constructed in 1856, it was 1,300 feet from water's edge, but within twenty years the shore had eroded to within 75 feet of the structure. The light was in operation until 1932, when it was decommissioned and deeded to the state. After World War II it was scheduled for demolition, but public outcry saved it. (Both the Absecon Lighthouse and the Barnegat Lighthouse were designed by George Meade, who was also the Union commander at the Battle of Gettysburg.) The Absecon Lighthouse is painted in distinctive colors, as are all lighthouses, to differentiate it from any other; in this case, it is white with a red band at the center.

Atlantic City

The Absecon Lighthouse in Atlantic City

Ventnor, Atlantic City's nearest neighbor to the south, would have been part of the city, but a narrow inlet existed between them in the 1880s, when the railroad came through and the building boom started. As the years passed, this inlet slowly began filling in and was finally dubbed Dry Inlet. It is now Jackson Avenue.

Eight miles south of Absecon Inlet, at the south end of Absecon Island, is Great Egg Harbor Inlet, which enters through the barrier islands just north of Ocean City (chart 7.2). The Ferris wheel at Ocean City makes it easily identifiable from offshore. Ocean City's Great Egg Harbor Inlet is reasonably safe in calm to moderate conditions but is subject to continual change and shoaling. The entrance buoys, which are uncharted, are shifted frequently to mark the best water, as storms continually rearrange the bottom. The inlet is used mainly by local boats, but a visit there is well worth it, and there are several large marina complexes that welcome transients located beyond the bascule bridge and next to the Intracoastal Waterway.

When entering any inlet, it's good to remember that breakers are the primary threat. It is much easier to see breakers when one is heading out of an inlet than it is when one is heading in. This is because, on the seaward side of a breaker, the crest of the wave hides the white foam of the breaking face; a more attentive and intuitive attitude is required.

Great Egg Harbor Inlet, Ocean City

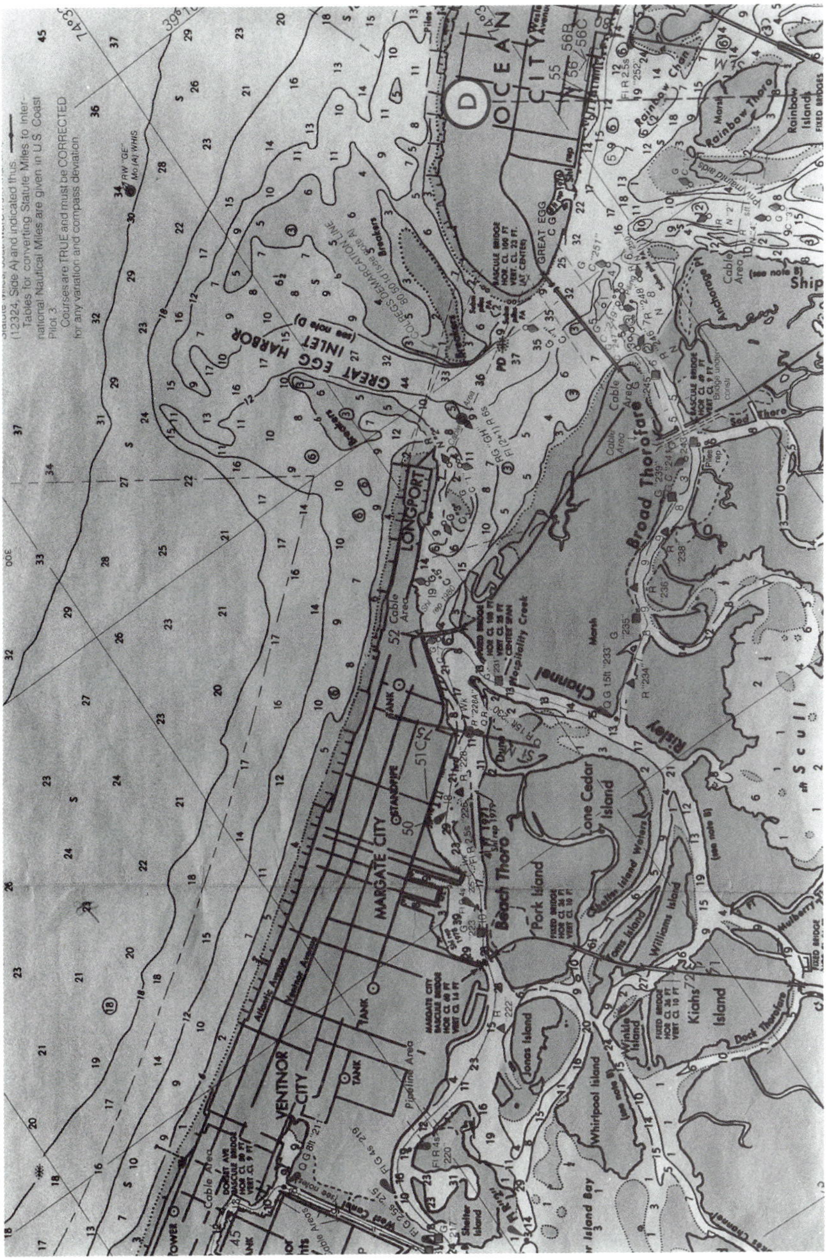

Chart 7.2 Great Egg Harbor Inlet and Ocean City (reproduced from NOAA's Chart #12316)

When planning to stay at Ocean City for a day or more, be sure to visit Ocean City's beach, which is superb. The Great Egg Coast Guard Station is in a small basin just south of the bridge. It can be reached on Ch-16 or Ch-22A.

Often, when looking at the charts of this area, people wonder why Great Egg Harbor is smaller than Little Egg Harbor, which is located further to the north. The answer lies in the size of the eggs rather than in the size of the bays. The early explorers, when pilfering eggs from the nests of sea birds, discovered the eggs to be bigger on the smaller harbor to the south.

Fourteen miles further southwest along the shore one will find Corsons Inlet, which is not recommended for the stranger under any circumstances. The inlet is not buoyed, and breakers are across the entire opening.

Twenty miles south of Atlantic City, and just north of Avalon, one comes to Townsends Inlet, which is just slightly less dangerous than Corsons Inlet. As with all of New Jersey's so-called unimproved inlets, entrance buoys are not charted. The bascule bridge directly across Townsends Inlet has a closed clearance of 23 feet, and the ICW is just inside the bridge. Shoaling has been reported under the bridge that can create swirling currents during tide changes. It's important to know that the Coast Guard station inside Townsends Inlet is only in operation during the summer months. From off the shore of Avalon, on a clear day, one can see the high rises of Atlantic City in the distance.

Townsends Inlet, Avalon

Several years ago, when sailing along this section of coastline, we had our first and only encounter with a *microburst*. The microburst, a recently recognized meteorological phenomenon, is a blast of hurricane-force wind that only lasts a few seconds and is out of proportion to the prevailing wind conditions. They occur when cloud conditions are just right, even in apparently fine weather. Old-time sailors called them "white squalls." It is theorized that microbursts have been the cause of plane crashes and that they have sent many ships and small boats to the bottom. The phenomenon has been cited as the probable cause for the sinking of *The Pride of Baltimore* and of the *Cutty Sark* replica, as well as of many other substantial and well-built boats, both power and sail.

When we had our microburst experience, Elsie and I were sailing close to shore, with every stitch of sail flying—the wind all day had not exceeded ten knots. Suddenly and without warning, we were struck by a blast of a sixty- to seventy-knot wind for five to ten seconds. Our boat is "stiff"; it is hard to get the rail wet on the windiest of days. The boat was immediately laid over, and we had solid water on the deck. Although I was afraid the water might go into the open portholes, the wind was back to ten knots before I was able to roundup and was gentle for the rest of the day.

If you hug the shoreline when traveling south, as we were doing that day, you'll notice that the coastline at Avalon juts out about a mile farther than does the coastline to the north. Shoaling extends for an additional three-quarters of a mile beyond that so, if you're traveling close to shore, a detour well offshore is mandatory.

Twenty-eight miles south from Atlantic City, and just north of Wildwood, you'll come to Hereford Inlet. Due to the constantly changing shoals and breakers that are present here at all times, strangers should not attempt the passage. The shoal waters at the mouth of the inlet extend a good mile offshore, and at low tide there is a sandbar awash, locally known as "champagne island."

The historic and attractive Hereford Inlet Lighthouse, which is only 46 feet high, is hard to find from offshore. It went into service in 1874 and, after a severe 1913 storm, it was undermined and finally moved 150 feet west. The unusual Victorian-style lighthouse, which is open to the public, is in a two-story building that is topped by the light tower. It was taken over by the city of North Wildwood in 1982, and its restoration has been undertaken by a group of local citizens, members of the Hereford Inlet Lighthouse Commission.

If a visit to the Wildwoods is on the schedule they can be reached more safely by entering Cape May Inlet further to the south and then by taking the Intracoastal Waterway north. Bridges on this short inland passage between Cape May Inlet and the Wildwoods are bascule, so that even sailboats can make the trip. When one is offshore of Wildwood on a clear day, the 641-foot Loran

Hereford Inlet, Wildwood

Wildwood

The Loran tower at Cape May

tower can be easily seen; it's located about one-third of a mile inland, on the north side of Cape May Inlet and serves as a good landmark.

Cape May Inlet was formerly listed on the charts by its original name, Cold Spring Harbor Inlet; but, since nobody ever called it that, NOAA has finally dropped the appellation, and it is now shown on the charts as Cape May Inlet. This deep, nearly all-weather inlet, is enclosed by breakwaters and leads into the harbor of Cape May, where marinas, stores, and restaurants abound within either walking or biking distance. Just inside the Cape May Inlet, the New Jersey Intracoastal Waterway system comes to an end, where the Cape May Inlet, the Cape May Harbor, and the ICW merge. A trip down Cape May's harbor brings us to the Cape May Canal, which gives access to Delaware Bay for boats that are able to pass under the two fixed bridges (55-foot clearance).

Skippers of boats with masts over 55 feet, and those who elect to remain offshore and enter Delaware Bay from the ocean, should approach the shallow waters at the tip of Cape May with caution. The joining of Delaware Bay and the Atlantic is strewn with shoals: Prissy Wicks, Overfalls, McCrie, Five Fathom Bank, and others (chart 7.3). If one has local knowledge, a transit around the tip of the cape can be made a few hundred yards offshore. Note that on either side of this passage, depths at low tide can be two feet. A stranger to the area would be safer entering Cape May Channel from about 4 miles offshore, at around the

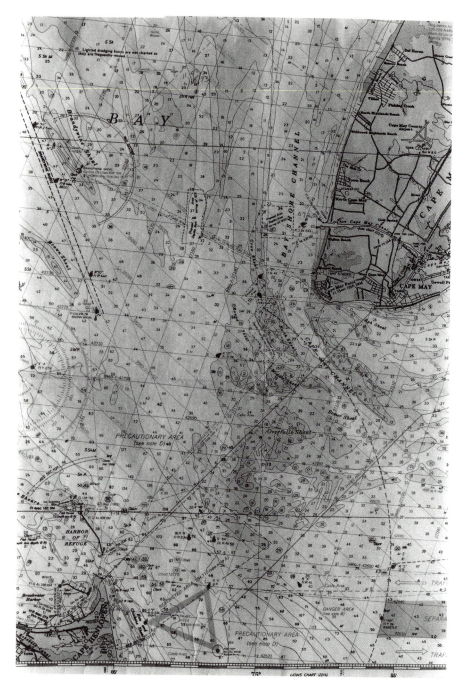

Chart 7.3 The mouth of Delaware Bay between Cape May and Cape Henlopen (reproduced from NOAA's Chart #12304)

eastern end of Prissy Wicks Shoal. Of the various offshore entrances from the ocean into Delaware Bay, the most conservative approach is probably by way of the large-ship channel just to the north of Cape Henlopen, Delaware. The ocean sands along this southern tip of New Jersey are constantly shifting, and the buoys are frequently uncharted because of their constant relocation. Even the charted buoys may not be where they're expected.

Whether by the intracoastal route or the offshore route, we have now reached New Jersey's southeastern corner, Cape May, where we will stop over before cruising New Jersey's southern coast, the Delaware Bay.

In the next chapter we'll explore Delaware Bay and its tributaries, from Cape May to the mouth of the Delaware River, at the juncture of the Chesapeake and Delaware Canal.

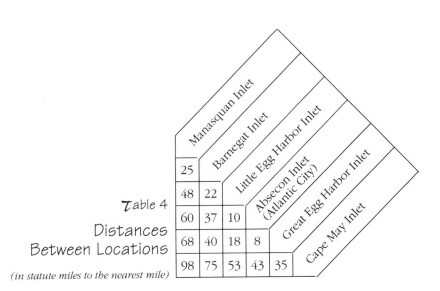

Table 4

Distances
Between Locations

(in statute miles to the nearest mile)

	Manasquan Inlet	Barnegat Inlet	Little Egg Harbor Inlet	Absecon Inlet (Atlantic City)	Great Egg Harbor Inlet	Cape May Inlet
Barnegat Inlet	25					
Little Egg Harbor Inlet	48	22				
Absecon Inlet (Atlantic City)	60	37	10			
Great Egg Harbor Inlet	68	40	18	8		
Cape May Inlet	98	75	53	43	35	

Chapter Eight

Delaware Bay and Its Tributaries

*O*f all the navigable tide water along the east coast Delaware Bay is probably the least known and least loved. It is one of the few places along the Atlantic coast where cruising skippers can find themselves completely alone and, at times, out of sight of land, even though on inland waters. The 50-mile, nearly straight line up the bay from the Cape May Canal to the Chesapeake and Delaware Canal (hereafter referred to as the C&D), is considered a chore, to be quickly navigated. The uninhabited shore can appear bleak and generally devoid of scenic variety. The green and brown expanse of low marshlands possesses few towns, marinas, or other signs of life, except for migratory birds in the air overhead, muskrats on shore, and a few fishers, crabbers, or oysterers off the channel. In the main channel yachts must share the water with giant commercial vessels that serve the commercial ports on the Delaware River and on the northern Chesapeake Bay.

Normal tide ranges of about five to six feet create a one to two knot tidal flow, and seas in these relatively shallow waters can build into a steep, short chop, with buoys out of sight even in clear weather, and few obvious places of refuge.

Most skippers crossing the bay pick up a feeling of emptiness and loneliness. No wonder they want to complete the trip across the bay as soon as possible. To others, though, the bay provides a sense of tranquility and solitude. It may be one of the few stretches on any of New Jersey's inland waters where the cruising skipper can experience the solitary existence of the offshore sailor and feel charged with a lone responsibility and independence not felt along the populated shores that make up the rest of the state's coastline. Skippers who are confident of their skills and willing to test them find the bay interesting to explore, and its very remoteness a balm to the soul. The sparse landscape invites reflection.

⚓ ⚓

Instead of a featureless shoreline, the interested boater sees marshlands teeming with life. The yellow grass, *spartina patens,* also called salt grass, along the shoreline, is a sanctuary to millions of migratory birds, whose flight paths range from Argentina to the Canadian tundra. On the bay, oysterers are at work trying to restore their prolific industry, and fishers fish the bay or use it as an access to Atlantic waters. On our last trip, near the mouth of the bay, we sighted a pilot whale, and on nearly every cruise in recent years we have been joined by dolphin, giving evidence that the bay's long history of pollution may finally be reversing.

The eastern end of the bay joins the Atlantic between Cape May, New Jersey, to the north, and Cape Henlopen, Delaware, on the south. The waters here can be, alternately, a formidable foe or a calm and tranquil friend.

The waters and shores of Delaware Bay have experienced only limited changes since their discovery by European explorers. In the early 1600s, about the same time the *Mayflower* landed at Cape Cod, Dutch explorer Cornelius Mey, traversing the coast in his ship *Fortune,* modestly named the two capes after himself. The southern cape became Cape Cornelius and the northern cape, Cape Mey. "Hindelopen," also named in honor of a Dutch mariner, designated the area south of Cape Cornelius. This name, becoming Henlopen, was finally used to designate the entire area of the southern cape while, with a slight spelling change, May came to designate the northern cape.

Well before the Dutch, Swedish, and English explorers traveled through the area, Native Americans paddled across the 17 miles of sea between the tips of the two capes in their flimsy canoes.

In modern times, the trip was made easier with a ferry service between the capes, but not until 1964, after lengthy negotiations between authorities from New Jersey and Delaware. The Cape May–Lewes Ferry provides access to the Delmarva peninsula to those heading south by car, by bike, or on foot, while Atlantic City gambling facilities can be reached by ferry customers heading north from such places as Delaware, Maryland, and Virginia.

As with nearly all the estuaries along the Atlantic Coast, Delaware Bay and the Delaware River have always been strategically important during wartime, from as far back as the Revolution. During the War of 1812, the British blockaded the mouth of the Delaware River in an effort to close down the Port of Philadelphia and, during the First World War, Delaware Bay was a site of conflict. In May of 1918, the German submarine U-151, very low on supplies, entered Delaware Bay. Because of the shallow bay waters the submarine operated on the surface. It intercepted three schooners, confiscated their food and supplies, and took all three twenty-six-member crews prisoner. Finally, TNT charges were placed on board the schooners and ignited, sending the ships to

The Cape May–Lewes Ferry

the bottom of the bay. The U-151 crew members then laid mines across the mouth of the bay and sank thirteen ships in the waters off New Jersey and New York before heading back to Germany.

Today, as we head across Delaware Bay in our schooner, the waters look so tranquil that it's hard to believe they were the scene of such conflict.

Small boats that leave Cape May harbor destined for the Delaware Bay crossing, have access to the bay via the Cape May Canal; it starts at the southwestern tip of Cape May Harbor and cuts across the southern end of the cape to the Delaware Bay (chart 8.1). Unfortunately, very large sailboats will be prevented from using this route by the two 55-foot fixed bridges crossing the canal. The only alternative is to go out through the Cape May Inlet and enter Delaware Bay from the ocean.

For the majority of boats, the Cape May Canal is the easiest answer. Tidal flow in the canal seldom reaches two and a half knots, which is generally not a problem on this short run. Halfway down the canal, just before the second fixed highway bridge, one will pass a railroad swing bridge, which is rusted into the open position. There is a six knot speed limit in the canal to prevent excessive erosion along the nonbulkheaded banks.

At the western end of the canal, just before emerging into Delaware Bay, one encounters the terminal for the Cape May–Lewes Ferry. If any ferry traffic is

Chart 8.1 Cape May Inlet, Harbor, and Canal (reproduced from NOAA's Chart #12316)

The Cape May Canal

The Cape May–Lewes Ferry terminal near the western end of the Cape May Canal

seen either leaving or arriving, it would be wise to wait for it to clear. Ferries create large wakes between the entrance breakwaters and also turbulence in the canal; when turning, a ferry takes up the whole waterway. The presence of this terminal provides a benefit on the return trip, since the large white fuel tank near the ferry terminal can be seen for miles and provides an excellent land-mark when one is searching for the entrance to the Cape May Canal.

Before starting a trip across Delaware Bay, we always check the VHF weather channel so we'll know what to expect. The Delaware Bay can change its personality within an hour. Northwest and southeast winds, along the axis of the bay, can cause a high, short chop; and gale winds from either of these directions can build seas to ten feet or more near the mouth of the bay. During the summer months the prevailing southerly winds are reinforced by a sea breeze, and seas tend to build as the day progresses. Visibility is generally good, but during the spring and early summer (April, May, and June), advection fog is common, reducing visibility to a boat length. These fogs often lift as the day progresses, especially close to the shore. Fog is much less likely to be encoun-tered during July, August, and September.

Once within the bay proper, water depth, at least for the recreational boat, is not a major concern. But, there are numerous shoals at the entrance to the

The Delaware Bay entrance to the Cape May Canal

bay. These created problems as far back as 1609, when Henry Hudson was looking for the Northwest Passage. He entered Delaware Bay in his eighty-ton ship, the *Half Moon,* and promptly ran aground, probably having struck one of the shoals. In the ship's log Hudson wrote: "He that will thoroughly discover this great bay must have a small Pinnace, that must draw but four or five feet of water, to sound before him."

Most small boats that traverse the bay between the Cape May and the C&D canals avoid the main channel where the large ships navigate. This channel is 1,000 feet wide in the bay and 400 feet wide on the Delaware River, leading to Philadelphia and Camden. There is plenty of water for small craft outside this channel, so small boats can avoid competing with heavy shipping. A nearly straight-line course from canal to canal also avoids travel in the roughest waters of the bay; it is locally called "going across the flats." A rhumb-line course between the Cape May Canal and Ship John Shoal Lighthouse, just south of the Cohansey River (317° true), will take recreational craft well away from Brandywine Shoal. Brandywine Shoal is west of the Cape May Canal and east of the Brandywine Range main channel. This straight-line route across the bay will also bypass Cross Ledge shoal, where the ruins of an abandoned lighthouse can be seen on its southeastern edge. Cross Ledge shoal is west of Egg Island Point and just east of the main channel.

Along this route skippers will encounter some recreational and commercial fishing boats and crab-pot buoys, as well as frequent vertical PVC pipes that mark oyster beds.

Although the direct route from the Cape May Canal to Ship John Shoal Lighthouse is the only part of Delaware Bay seen by most transient boaters, there are many other interesting options.

When leaving the Cape May Canal, if one heads north instead of crossing the bay, the route will lead to the Maurice (pronounced Morris) River (chart 8.2). In the 1630s a Dutch ship, *The Maurice,* named for the Prince of Orange-Nassau in the Netherlands was captured by Indians and burned near the mouth of this river, giving the river its name.

The Maurice River was also the center of activity for Delaware Bay's oyster fleet from the early 1700s until 1957, when a parasitic blight destroyed most of the oyster beds. Prior to the 1957 blight, Delaware Bay was the source of oysters for major East Coast cities. Almost overnight the rich oyster beds suffered such damage that they were nearly annihilated. The appropriately named towns of Bivalve and Shellpile, on the Maurice River, were once home to between five and six hundred oyster schooners and other sailing vessels, and oysters were shipped from Bivalve's railroad terminal. The oyster industry in the bay is still trying to make a comeback.

Rutgers University researchers are currently working at the Haskin Shellfish

A restored World War II PT-boat on Delaware Bay

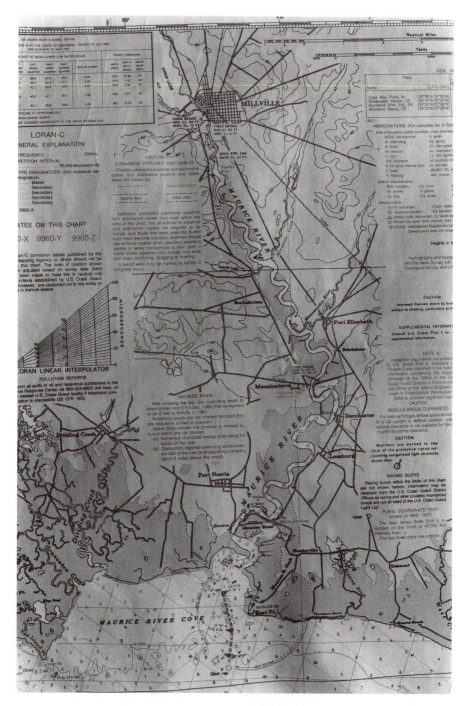

Chart 8.2 The Maurice River (reproduced from NOAA's Chart #12304)

Research Lab in Port Norris, located on the Maurice River (under grants from the U.S. Commerce Department), seeking to develop a disease-resistant hybrid of the American and Pacific oyster. The hybrid would be resistant to the two oyster-killing parasites, Dermo and MSX (neither of which is harmful to humans), which were responsible for the 1957 devastation.

In December 1993, President Clinton designated 37 miles of the Maurice River and three of its tributaries—the Muskee, Menantico, and Manumuskin creeks—as part of the National Wild and Historic Scenic Rivers System. The legal implication of this designation is to preserve the waterway and to regulate future development along its banks. In recent years ospreys have returned to the Maurice River, nearly a dozen families, as well as more than sixteen bald eagles, which hunt up and down the river.

The head of navigation on the Maurice River is at Millville, where the 898-acre Lake Union empties into the river. The lake was created by a dam across the river that backs the water up for almost four miles. It is a pretty setting, with small islands and high banks to the west, but due to asbestos contamination, the lake has been closed for a cleanup, which is expected to be completed in 1997. South of the lake the river is tidal, while on the river north of the lake, the waters are a canoeing and kayaking delight (see *Exploring the Little Rivers of New Jersey*, by Cawley and Cawley, Rutgers University Press, 1993).

When heading for the Maurice River, look out for the red-roofed East Point Lighthouse on the east side of the entrance; it's a daytime marker that can be seen far down the bay. Built in 1849 on a jut of land once known as Dead Man's Shoal, it's purpose was to keep ships from grounding at this point as well as to provide a navigational landmark identifying the entrance into the Maurice River. The lighthouse was in operation until 1941. The two and a half story brick structure has a cupola on top where the beacon was housed; it is now owned by the Maurice River Historical Society.

Buoys mark the channel entrance to the Maurice River, where boats of less than 5 foot draft can cross the entrance bar at low tide. Here, as with most of New Jersey's tidewaters, strong winds can change water depths considerably. This also holds true for other streams off Delaware Bay, where blow-in and blow-out tides can affect water depth across the entrance bars. The marked channel into the Maurice River passes east of Fowler Island, which is in the middle of the river's mouth. Beyond the entrance bar, the river runs very deep through flat marshlands. Visitors can anchor behind the island, at the mouth of the river, or farther up the river, off the channel. When anchoring, allow for the 6-foot tide. Port Norris Marina and Robinson's Oyster Farm, located on the west bank, offer slips for transients and repair services.

In Port Norris a reclamation project is under way to restore the schooner

Clyde A. Phillips, built in New Jersey in 1928. A dedicated network of volunteers is undertaking the project, which was begun in 1988. The restoration project is a ponderous task, as rotten planks and ribs must be removed and replaced with new wood. The proposed plans are for the schooner to sail from port to port on the bay as a floating classroom that is expected to carry 15,000 passengers annually.

Farther up the river, on both banks, other boat yards, like the majority of those on the Maurice River, cater to the commercial fisher. Some may be able to supply dock space to the recreational boater. The river continues to snake through the wetlands for twenty miles before reaching the head of navigation at Millville, where land along the river is being converted to waterfront parks, with boat ramps, fishing piers, and Little League ballparks.

Both the New Jersey and Delaware shorelines of Delaware Bay are marshlands, so remember, when either anchored out or in a marina during the summer months, screening is a necessity. What this part of the world lacks in flora, it more than makes up for in tiny fauna. The greenhead fly, which inhabits the coastal marshlands from Georgia north, can be troublesome during the day; mosquitoes become bothersome at around sunset; and on windless days, no-see-ums can be annoying.

As one heads west from the Maurice River, along the marshlands on the northern shoreline of the bay, Egg Island Point provides a good landmark. West of the point, the harbor town of Fortescue is home to a large fishing fleet. Facilities for transients are nearly nonexistent here, and the State Marina, one of several marinas in Fortescue, lists only one dock space for transients. The entrance into the harbor at Fortescue has about 4 feet at low water, and there is a sharp turn just inside the mouth. During the summer months the Coast Guard operates a search-and-rescue team out of Fortescue. There are several marinas in the basin, and restaurants are within walking distance.

Along the shore, about six miles northwest of Fortescue, the thirty-foot tower, with a six-second flashing light at Ben Davis Point, marks the entrance to Back Creek, which can be used as a storm shelter. There are no facilities here, but the creek has navigable water for about two miles upstream.

When we find the weather rapidly deteriorating, or when a shower and meal ashore are in order, we frequently take a detour into the Cohansey River, whose entrance is located about two nautical miles north of Ship John Shoal Lighthouse. This lighthouse, one of the oldest on the bay, is located about midway between the Cape May and C&D canals. Ship John Shoal Lighthouse is surrounded by riprap and is easily visible for miles. (The lighthouse was built on the shoal where the ship *John* went aground in December of 1797.)

The Cohansey is by far the most convenient and safest harbor of refuge for boats traveling between the two canals, since it is not far off the main channel. The tower on the entrance island, at the mouth of the Cohansey, can be easily confused with several other towers along this section of the shoreline. When heading from Ship John Shoal Lighthouse, use red nun buoy number ten, which marks Dunks Shoal as a good checkpoint. Better yet, a Loran or a GPS fix can confirm the entrance, which is about a quarter of a mile northwest from the skeletal entrance tower.

Although the entrance into the river can be made on either side of the entrance island, the dredged cut northwest of the island, on which the tower stands, is preferred. We leave the unmarked entrance on the other side of the island to the locals.

Once inside the entrance, one will find that this deep stream meanders with indecision through the meadowlands; it is navigable all the way to Bridgeton, about seventeen miles above the mouth of the river (chart 8.3). Although Bridgeton is the seat of Cumberland County, there are no docking facilities available there.

About three miles up from the mouth of the river, on the north bank, there are two marinas situated a few hundred yards apart. Both usually have space

The Ship John Shoal Lighthouse

available for transients and deep water at dockside. The first marina, Hancock's Harbor, offers gas, diesel, and a few supplies, as well as showers and a home-style restaurant that is popular with the locals. The restaurant is closed on Monday and Tuesday. After a rough day on the bay it is a refreshing place to stop, clean up, and get away from the galley.

The second marina, Ship John Inn and Marina, has dockage for transients, diesel, gas, showers, washers and dryers, a travel lift, and it is capable of providing major repair services. It has a marine store that stocks a large variety of engine parts and marine supplies, which can usually provide for most of our basic on-board needs. The Ship John Inn, adjacent to the marina, offers cocktails, supper and, frequently, live entertainment. It, too, is closed on Monday and Tuesday.

The nearby residential town of Greenwich (pronounced "green-which"), about a mile from the northern marina, was the scene of New Jersey's version of the Boston Tea Party in December 1774 (a year after the event in Boston). In Greenwich, the tea was off-loaded from the brig *Greyhound,* which was anchored in the Cohansey. It was seized by protesters, who were dressed as American Indians, and burned in an open field.

From the Ship John Marina, the one mile walk or bike ride into the town of Greenwich takes one up Pier Road to a right turn on Market Street, and then a

Chart 8.3 The Cohansey River (reproduced from NOAA's Chart #12304)

The Hancock Harbor Marina on the Cohansey River near Greenwich

Our schooner, *Delphinus*, at the Ship John Marina

left turn on Ye Greate Street. The Greenwich General Store and Historical Society will be found to the right, and a little further along, on the left, one will come to the Maritime Museum. The general store has nearly everything one needs for a restocking of the galley, and the town's post office is located in the same building.

If we decide on anchoring out for the night on the Cohansey, we either anchor off the channel near one of the bends in the river or behind the entrance island. Anchoring in this deep river requires lots of anchor rode, since inside the entrance bar the river runs very deep. Recently, to escape a strong wind and heavy seas on the bay, we anchored just beyond the first bend in the river. We had 200 feet of anchor line out and still couldn't get a 6:1 scope.

When anchoring in any of the rivers off Delaware Bay, or when approaching a dock at one of the marinas, be aware that there is a nominal six-foot tide. At the height of tide changes, the water doesn't saunter—it races. Before approaching a dock, first determine the tide flow and then make the approach into the flow for maximum control. Floating docks are the norm, helping to keep fenders properly positioned. When a planned departure time for the next day is fixed, it is a good idea to calculate tide flow beforehand. If it will be coming from astern, and if it appears there might be problems when leaving the dock, we turn our boat around at the next convenient slack water and sleep better that night. This precaution can be especially important for auxiliaries, whose power is limited and whose underwater configuration is more readily affected by tidal flow—and I speak from experience.

When leaving the Cohansey and heading up the bay, be sure to go around red nun buoy number 10, marking the end of Dunks Bar. As one travels farther up the bay, the shorelines of Delaware and New Jersey are closer together, where Delaware Bay becomes Delaware River.

The demarcation line between bay and river wasn't established until 1905, when the New Jersey and Delaware legislatures created a commission to draw the line. This arbitrary and imaginary line, 42 miles above the Delaware capes, runs between the southern entrance to Hope Creek, New Jersey, and Liston Point, Delaware. Stone markers on both shores make it official. In spite of the official demarcation line, boaters usually consider the bay to be between the C&D and Cape May canals.

Farther up the bay, the twin domes of the Salem Nuclear Power Plant on Artificial Island are prominently shown on the government charts; the plant's huge cooling tower, with water vapor emanating from the top, dominates the landscape. This type of tower is used to cool the water from the turbine generators, and engineers call this strange shape a hyperbolic cooling tower, after the geometric curves used in its design. This nuclear facility is operated by Public

The nuclear plants on Artificial Island

Service Electric and Gas Company. The two domes shown on the chart are separate nuclear reactors, Salem-1 and Salem-2. These reactors, built by Westinghouse and plagued with problems in recent years, began service in 1977. When operating properly, they can supply more than 2 billion watts of electricity, enough for 2 million homes.

Not shown on the 1992 chart is the third reactor dome, that of the newer Hope Creek Nuclear Plant, built by G.E. It's just a few hundred feet from the Salem plant domes. The Hope Creek Nuclear Plant, which went into service in 1987, is a stellar performer that receives little publicity.

Between Artificial Island, location of the nuclear plants, and the channel, there is a designated anchorage area for commercial craft and barges. Located in this anchorage are black, steel anchor buoys, which are nearly submerged and easily missed—especially when the tide is running, or in a rough chop, or in fog. If you plan a shortcut through this anchorage, keep a sharp lookout.

Magnetic variations of up to five degrees have been noted on this part of the river, from Artificial Island all the way up the river to Marcus Hook, Pennsylvania, and these have existed long before the nuclear age. At the north end of Artificial Island, the boundary agreement between New Jersey and Delaware specifies that the river between this point and the Pennsylvania state line is entirely within the state of Delaware, the boundary between the two states being the high-tide mark on the New Jersey shoreline.

North of Artificial Island and on the west shore of the Delaware River is the entrance to the Chesapeake and Delaware Canal, the C&D, which joins the Delaware River with the north end of Chesapeake Bay.

On the other side of the river from the C&D, one will find two marinas on the Salem River. They are the distance of a long walk, a bike trip, or a cab ride from the town of Salem. (The old town of Salem, settled by the Quakers in 1675, has a rich history.)

The entrance to the Salem River is by way of buoyed channel markers running north-northeast. No shortcuts here! Shoal water is on both sides of the channel at low tide, but once inside, the Salem River runs deep. As one travels up the Salem River, the Penn Salem Marina is on the left. One can also take the cut at the Salem River entrance, and just after the cut, the Salem Boat Basin is to the right.

Once in the Salem area, the traveler has the choice of heading west to the Chesapeake Bay by way of the C&D or north up the Delaware River to the head of navigation near Trenton.

In the next and final chapter, we'll continue our cruise up the western water boundary of New Jersey, the Delaware River, to the head of navigation at Trenton.

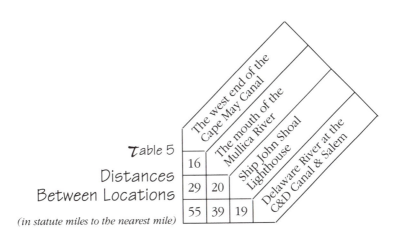

Table 5

Distances
Between Locations

(in statute miles to the nearest mile)

Chapter Nine

The Delaware River to Trenton

The Delaware River is bounded near its mouth by the states of New Jersey and Delaware, and farther north it runs between Pennsylvania and New Jersey, up to the tri-state rock that's located in the river near Port Jervis, New York. North of Port Jervis, at Hancock, New York, the river separates into the east and west branches, and these branches originate as small, clear, sparkling streams out of the Catskill Mountains in upstate New York. From its origins in the Catskills to its confluence with Delaware Bay, the river runs free for 330 miles, but the head of navigation is near Trenton, at the so-called falls, and our cruise will take us up the river to that point.

The Delaware River is like three different rivers: the clear, unspoiled northern headwaters, where it's a shallow river of rapids and white water flowing through woods and farmland; the busy industrial central section, where it's a major petroleum center for the east coast; and the wide estuary at the south, where the river combines with and loses its identity in Delaware Bay.

The lower Delaware River is a major commercial waterway. Its origin as a route for merchandising and barter began in the early seventeenth century, when the Dutch East India Company began establishing trading posts along its banks.

The earliest Dutch maps of the Delaware River employ the name *Suydt,* or south, to differentiate it from the North River, or the Hudson.

In 1681 William Penn, son of an admiral, was given a grant from the crown for lands west of the Delaware River. The northern section of these lands was named Pennsylvania, and after the Revolution, a hundred years later, the southern section was named Delaware. When William Penn first arrived at this primitive land in his ship *Welcome,* he landed north of where the Schuylkill joins the Delaware, where the water was deep right up to shore. Penns Landing, as it was later named, is located at the site that is now Philadelphia. There, in the proverbial middle of nowhere, Penn discovered that the Blue Anchor Tavern was already doing a thriving business.

⚓ ⚓

Naturally, in the 1700s there were no bridges across this wide section of the lower Delaware, below Trenton. This didn't deter the American Indians, who had been navigating and crossing the river for thousands of years on log rafts, canoes, and inflated animal intestines.

With the arrival of the Europeans, large ships traveled the river, which was now used as a highway for business, commerce, and colonization. The principal commercial product of the area in colonial times was flour, and the streams flowing into the Delaware, such as the Schuylkill, provided the water power to grind it. In those early years, water-borne cargo was threatened by attack; privateers, American Indians, and pirates marauded Delaware Bay from Cape Henlopen to the lower Delaware River. One of the priates was Edward Teach, or Blackbeard, who was so bold as to buy his supplies in Philadelphia, well aware that the Quaker pacifists would do him no harm.

Across the river from Salem, New Jersey, at the southern end of the Delaware River, is the entrance to the Chesapeake and Delaware Canal, the 12-mile-long canal that joins the Delaware River with the north end of Chesapeake Bay (chart 9.1). The C&D, first proposed in 1661 by Dutch cartographer Augustine Herman, became a pet project of Benjamin Franklin's after the Revolution. Construction of a narrow waterway was begun, and the canal was finally opened in 1829.

The canal has changed considerably since those early days of mule power

The Delaware River entrance to the C&D Canal

Chart 9.1 The C&D Canal, Salem River, and Pea Patch Island (reproduced from NOAA's Chart #12311)

and locks, and today it is a wide, lock-free, easily navigated waterway, 450 feet wide, that can handle major shipping. Red flashing traffic lights at each end of the canal indicate when the canal is closed, and the dispatcher at Chesapeake City reports conditions every thirty minutes on Ch-13. When transiting the canal, sailboats must use auxiliary power, and anchoring in the canal is prohibited.

On the west shore of the Delaware River, two miles northwest of the C&D, one will find Delaware City, Delaware, which is a convenient place for reprovisioning. It is reached by taking Bulkhead Shoal Channel, to the south of Pea Patch Island, and by entering the Delaware City Branch Canal. At low tide the town dock near the entrance is suitable only for dinghies, but a little further on, just before the fixed bridge, one can try the Delaware City Marina. It usually has space for transients, and from here it is a couple of blocks into town, where there are two small grocery stores, a drugstore, a deli, a restaurant, a pizzeria, a liquor store, and antique shops.

There is also a ferry dock that provides passenger service to the Fort Delaware State Park on Pea Patch Island. The ferry operates on weekends and holidays, from the end of June to the end of September; and it also operates on Wednesday, Thursday, and Friday, from the middle of June to the beginning of September. The only dock for visiting boaters at Pea Patch Island is just beyond the ferry dock on the west side of the island, and it is only suitable for dinghies.

At the fort on Pea Patch Island, authentically clad guides take visitors back in time, to the days of the Civil War, and recount stories about the fort's role in history. There is a museum on the island, and observation platforms overlook the largest nesting site for wading birds on the East Coast.

As we cruise north on the Delaware from the junction of the C&D, New Castle Range takes us close to the eastern side of Pea Patch Island, home of the infamous Civil War prison, Fort Delaware, that has been called the Andersonville of the north. It is now part of the Delaware State Park system.

Construction of the granite fort on Pea Patch Island was begun in 1846. Six thousand wooden pilings were used for is foundation. It was completed in 1860 and was designed to protect the Delaware River to the north from Confederate attack. The fort's history was destined to be less than heroic. In spite of its intended role as a proud citadel charged with protecting the river north to Philadelphia, it was turned into a prison camp for Confederate soldiers and Union deserters. The first prisoners to arrive, from Stonewall Jackson's command, were lodged in the dungeons, and soon the camp housed more than 12,000 prisoners, making it the largest prison camp in the country. The fort was ill-suited to its purpose. The prisoners were malnourished and plagued with disease, and a large percentage of both the prisoners and the Union garrison died. The dead are buried at the Fort Mott Civil War burial ground at Finns Point,

Fort Delaware on Pea Patch Island

located on the New Jersey shore directly east of Pea Patch Island. A monument at Finns Point is a miniature reproduction of the Washington Monument that commemorates the 2,436, mostly unknown, Confederate soldiers who died while imprisoned on Pea Patch Island. Each year, on April 26, the Daughters of the Confederacy hold a wreath ceremony at the site. There is also a smaller monument to the 135 members of the Union garrison who died.

There are no docks at Finns Point; however, there is reasonably deep water off the channel for anchoring. Double-check the chart first so that you don't anchor in the underwater cable area between the mainland and Pea Patch Island. A dinghy can be taken to the sandy shore-beach, but keep an eye out for the nearly buried remains of granite groins that were put in to stabilize the shoreline.

There are now plans for a recreational pier to be built into the Delaware at Fort Mott. When it is completed it will be included as a stop for the ferry that now takes visitors from Delaware City, Delaware, to Pea Patch Island. The target date for the pier's completion is Fort Mott's centennial in 1996.

The fortifications of Fort Mott, which was named for New Jersey native General Gershom Mott, are just across the open field from the river bank. The Civil War burial ground and monuments are nearly a mile away.

Although the three-fort defense system for this part of the Delaware River

The Confederate Soldiers' monument at Finns Point

The Union garrison's monument at Finns Point

was designed in 1794, the bulwarks now standing at Fort Mott date from 1896 and were built as Spanish-American War fortifications. They were never used.

During World War I, Pea Patch Island was pulled into another war effort. It was feared that the Port of Philadelphia and the ship-building and oil refineries to the south might come under attack so, during the summer of 1917, a net made of steel chains was designed as a U-boat deterrent. It was stretched across the river from Pea Patch Island to Finns Point. It couldn't, however, stand up to a fierce early winter storm that year, and it was swept away.

As we continue our trip up the Delaware River, we pass between historic Pea Patch Island, Delaware, and Finn's Point, New Jersey. At Finns Point the river makes an almost ninety degree bend toward the northeast, after which the state of Delaware is on both sides of the river. "Impossible," you might say; "New Jersey is on the east bank." It is true nonetheless. Although not shown on the nautical chart, an aberration in the original definition of the border between the states of New Jersey and Delaware causes the boundary line to cut through the Killcohook National Wildlife Refuge on the western tip of Finns Point, so that a large section of that shoreline belongs to the state of Delaware. This same anomaly causes the northern tip of Artificial Island, north of the nuclear plants, to be a part of Delaware. If you don't believe it, check a good road map or atlas for confirmation.

Finns Point is the home of one of New Jersey's least known yet most historic lighthouses, built to mark the sharp turn in the river and used as an artillery observation post. It was built in 1876, and it is hard to see from the river. After its restoration in the 1980s, it was added to the National Register of Historic Places.

On the lower Delaware River and the upper Delaware Bay the various channels are termed ranges, and the buoys in these channels display a letter that denotes the range. Thus, buoys on the New Castle Range carry the suffix N, on the Deepwater Point Range a D, on the Cherry Island Range a C, and so on.

Delaware River tidal currents can have a significant effect on the speed-over-the-bottom of auxiliaries or other boats of displacement-hull design, and can cut the true speed almost in half. Further up the river, ebb tides are of an even greater velocity, since tidal currents and river flow are added together. As an example, the tides at New Castle, which are three and a half to four hours after those at the entrance to Delaware Bay, cause a 1.9 knot flood tide (going up river) and a 2.4 knot ebb tide (flowing down river.)

As we approach the industrialized section of the Delaware River, debris in the water increases, especially after heavy rainstorms. For those in search of a bucolic setting, this is not the place, but it is interesting. When looking up river, one can see the high twin bridges of the New Jersey Turnpike, the Delaware River Memorial Bridge. Since there are few small-craft facilities along this stretch

Heavy shipping vessels join us as we head up the Delaware River

The New Jersey Turnpike Bridge across the Delaware River emerges from fog

of the Delaware, it is good to know that up the Christina River at Wilmington, and completely out of sight, are recreational marinas. The Delaware-Pennsylvania border reaches the river just south of the Sun Oil refinery at Marcus Hook. At this point the boundary line between the states returns to midriver. Across from Marcus Hook an anchorage exists on the New Jersey side of the channel; it is for tankers awaiting their turn at the docks on the west side of the river. It is a good idea to monitor Ch-16 and Ch-13 and to keep a wary eye on ship movements when transiting this area.

Across the river from Marcus Hook, a long pier with a crane on its outer end extends far out into the river from the New Jersey shore—and it is not shown on the chart.

The second bridge crosses the Delaware between Chester, Pennsylvania, and Bridgeport, New Jersey. About four miles beyond this bridge there are small-craft facilities on the Pennsylvania shore behind the two-mile-long Little Tinicum Island, in the town of Essington, Pennsylvania. These marinas are just off the ends of the runways belonging to Philadelphia International Airport. Although it is a convenient place for refueling, it is not the quietest place to spend the night, since flights are landing or taking off overhead nearly every minute.

Infrequently, small waterspouts have occurred in this area, apparently resulting from a vortex created by the jet traffic. They have occasionally done

The Pennsylvania shore near Marcus Hook

damage to boat covers and bimini tops. On the positive side, the several marinas there have fuel, supplies, and haul-out, and can handle hull and engine repairs. In addition, Little Tinicum Island provides protection from river wakes.

Just north of the Philadelphia airport the Schuylkill River flows into the Delaware. The river was named by the Dutch, and translates to hidden creek. The Schuylkill River runs through the center of Philadelphia, and the area around its mouth, at the confluence of the Delaware, has become the center of the petroleum industry at the Port of Philadelphia as well as home to the Philadelphia Navy Shipyard. I have an old photograph of my father paddling a canoe through Philadelphia on the tree-lined Schuylkill in the late 1800s—it is hard to believe it's the same river.

By the 1940s and 1950s, and before the promulgation of stringent federal and state pollution regulations, the Delaware River in the Philadelphia and Camden vicinity was in poor shape from an ecological standpoint. Water quality had already begun declining as far back as the 1700s, only about one hundred years after Henry Hudson discovered the Delaware. Then, the biggest polluters on the waterway were ships and the activity on the wharves, but in the latter half of the 1800s ship building, manufacturing, oil refineries, and a massive population growth sent the water quality into a rapid decline. The problem was compounded during World War II, when the importance of shipbuilding and oil

Entrance to the Schuylkill River

production superceded that of the environment. All of the waste from the new industries, as well as sewage from the exploding population, were dumped into the river and its tributaries. The water quality was so bad that ships at dockside had paint stripped from their hulls by the corrosive mixture.

Something clearly had to be done, and it started with a New Jersey, New York, Pennsylvania, and Delaware advisory commission, The Interstate Commission on the Delaware River Basin. The newly implemented environmental laws enabled the commission to set up water standards and cleanup programs.

Now the river water quality is improving noticeably each year, and environmental advocacy groups such as the Watershed Association of the Delaware River and the Delaware Riverkeeper plan to continue the fight. The Delaware River is one of ten bodies of water nationwide that has a keeper. The Delaware Riverkeeper organization, affiliated with the American Littoral Society, has been working since 1988 to change the face of stewardship on the river through monitoring by volunteers from Hancock, New York, to Delaware Bay.

Although the river, in its industrial southern reaches, might seem devoid of aquatic life, shad use these waters as a pathway to the upper reaches of the Delaware River in New York State, where they spawn in the spring. Then the young shad, during their fall migration, swim down, past pipes that spew treated sewage and chemical waste into the water, past oil refineries, and past the wild marshes of Delaware Bay.

Just north of the Schuylkill, on the Pennsylvania shore, the impressive Philadelphia Navy Yard maintains ships of all descriptions at dockside or in drydock, with the Philadelphia skyline as a backdrop.

As one rounds the next bend in the river, one will see the Walt Whitman Bridge, which joins Philadelphia to Gloucester City, New Jersey. Farther upriver, beyond the Walt Whitman Bridge, the Ben Franklin Bridge joins Philadelphia and Camden.

In 1898 vacationers from both Philadelphia and Camden began using the newly completed fifty-five-mile long railroad link from Camden to Atlantic City. The trains regularly made the trip in fifty minutes, racing through the New Jersey Pine Barrens, with smoke billowing from their stacks at speeds of more than sixty miles per hour. (The round-trip fare at the time was one dollar.) A 1920 railroad report revealed that of the sixteen fastest trains in the world, thirteen were on the Camden-Atlantic City run.

On the Philadelphia waterfront, Penns Landing rivals New York's South Street Seaport. In the boat basin one will find an outstanding collection of historic ships: a World War II submarine, *Becuna;* a tug boat; Commodore Dewey's flagship from the 1898 battle of Manila Bay, the *Olympia;* the tall sailing ship *Gazela;* and Barnegat Lightship, which replaced Barnegat Lighthouse.

The Philadelphia Navy Yard at the juncture of the Schuylkill and Delaware Rivers

Penns Landing at Philadelphia

Penns Landing has an 80-slip marina for recreational boats of up to forty feet long, where dock space for transients is sometimes available. A water taxi from Penns Landing makes several regular stops at specific locations on both the Pennsylvania and New Jersey sides of the river, connecting Penns Landing with restaurants, marinas, and the aquarium across the river in Camden (chart 9.2). The water taxi can be reached on Ch-68, and an all-day pass, providing unlimited usage, is available for five dollars/four dollars for children.

At dockside in Penns Landing one will find the Philadelphia Maritime Museum, a multitiered, tree-lined outdoor amphitheater, where concerts and festivals are held, and a sculpture garden. The Philadelphia Maritime Museum offers workshops that teach the art of crafting small wooden boats. Courses are taught by shipwrights.

In the last few years Philadelphia has become a leading cruise-ship port, and frequently these ships will be docked at the Penns Landing pier, adding to the intriguing maritime atmosphere.

The *Riverbus,* a shuttle-ferry, provides a quick and pleasant passage between Penns Landing and the New Jersey State Aquarium across the river in Camden. The ferry runs every half-hour, and the 2,500-foot trip takes less than ten minutes.

There are other marinas in Philadelphia, located just south and north of the

Commodore Dewey's flagship *Olympia* at Penns Landing

Ben Franklin Bridge. To the south of the bridge and north of Penns Landing, the jointly owned Pier-3 Marina and Pier-5 Marina usually monitor Ch-16. Both marinas have slips for transients with laundry, showers, rest rooms, a deli, and a restaurant. Slips have water, electricity, and cable-TV. The marina is secured with locked entrance gates and digital access codes. Transient boats should make advance reservations for the $1.25/ft. slips, and a deposit for the first night may be required along with the reservation. From these marinas it is a short walk into what is sometimes called America's most historic square mile. A good place to begin is the Visitors Center on Chestnut and 3rd streets, close to Independence Hall and the Liberty Bell. Long lines can be expected at important historical sites during the height of the tourist season. Philadelphia's Center City, with shopping, restaurants, hotels, and banks, is also nearby.

The Pier-3 and Pier-5 marinas are established between existing piers that were formerly used for commercial shipping. These piers have been converted into condominiums, which overlook the marinas. Entrance into the marinas is by way of two right-angle turns, designed to reduce wakes from river traffic.

Just to the north of the Ben Franklin Bridge the Philadelphia Marine Center offers a 300-slip marina for boats up to 150 feet in length. It has a complete range of amenities including car rentals, cable-TV, telephone hookups at dock-

Chart 9.2 The Philadelphia–Camden area (reproduced from NOAA's Chart #12312)

The Riverbus from Penns Landing, approaching the Camden Aquarium

side, showers, and a laundromat. Marina security is established with a locked gate at the land entrance.

Across the river from Philadelphia, the $52 million dollar Thomas H. Kean State Aquarium at Camden is the biggest attraction on the Camden waterfront. The facility was funded by the New Jersey State Legislature and was opened in 1992. It rivals the aquarium at Baltimore's Inner Harbor. The huge main tank within the building contains over three-quarters of a million gallons of "sea water," which is made from tap water, salt, and trace elements. It is the largest aquarium tank in the United States, with the exception of the one located at EPCOT Center in Florida.

The first floor of the aquarium focuses on aquatic life from New Jersey waters, and the second floor features marine life from around the world. Other displays include cascading waterfalls, ocean surf, touch-tanks, and a trout stream. There is a one and a half acre park surrounding the aquarium, with an outside seal pool, and the Riverside Cafe is on the deck of the aquarium, overlooking the Delaware. The aquarium is open every day except Thanksgiving, Christmas, and New Year's. Admission is $9 for adults, $6 for children ages two to eleven, and $7.50 for older students with school identification and for senior citizens.

One will find Wiggins Park Camden County Marina adjoining Camden

The Camden Aquarium (photo courtesy of Linda Riley, the New Jersey State Aquarium at Camden)

The Camden Aquarium with the Ben Franklin Bridge in the background

The Wiggins Park Camden County Marina

Aquarium on the south. The marina has floating docks, round-the-clock security, water, electricity, a picnic area, and it monitors Ch-16 and Ch-68. This facility has transient, seasonal, monthly, daily, and even hourly rates (for those who would like to stop off by boat and visit the aquarium). The hourly rates are $7 for the first hour and $2 for each additional hour. If planning to stay overnight, one should arrive at the marina before closing time, since the gate surrounding the marina is then locked and only boaters with keys have access. The marina is in the form of a complete circle, with slips around its periphery and rolling lawns separating it from the aquarium. At the top of the hill, between the two, a brick commons surrounded by tables is used for picnics and provides a view of the river and of Philadelphia across the way.

Walt Whitman spent most of his time on the Delaware River and found the scene comprised of the Camden-Philadelphia ferry, the ferry operators, the river's waterfowl, and the "full-starr'd, blue-black night" one that "speak[s] no word, nothing to the intellect, yet so eloquent, so communicative to the soul."

Walt Whitman (1819–1892) spent the last eight years of his life in his home at 330 Mickle Boulevard in Camden. The house, purchased with the royalties from *Leaves of Grass*, was close enough to the river so that Whitman could watch the tall ships cruising by. His home was one of Camden's most important museums until it burned to the ground in September 1994. The city has recently allocated funds to build a memorial park, including a bronze statue of the poet, near the spot where his home once stood.

Back on board, after an interesting day or two ashore, we will often head north from the Philadelphia-Camden area. Here, the Delaware becomes slightly less industrialized on both shores. The main channel heads to the west of Petty Island, and just beyond is a ConRail railroad bridge with a lift span that has a charted down-clearance of 49 feet. The Betsy Ross Highway bridge is just beyond. Skippers of sailboats would be wise to call ahead to the ConRail bridge-tender on Ch-13 to request the actual bridge clearance.

Two miles farther upriver, owners of large sailboats should also note the 53-foot closed clearance of the bridge at Palmyra. In these upper parts of the Delaware River's navigable waters it is important to remember that freshets can raise river levels considerably higher than normal. Bridge boards on the abutments to bridges should be checked for real clearance before you commit to a passage. During March and April, due to melting snow and ice breakup, freshets can cause the river to rise as much as 10 to 20 feet above mean low water at Trenton, and even heavy summertime rainstorms can cause a 9-foot rise. The maximum recorded freshet rises have been 21.5 feet at Trenton, 19.5 feet at Bordentown, and 13 feet at Bristol.

In these reaches of the river the tides, especially at times of high water or when the tide is ebbing, are fast-flowing and an auxiliary or displacement hull will have a hard time making progress against them. For those operating auxiliary or displacement hulls, planning the trip in conjunction with a tide table would be wise.

Just above the Palmyra Bridge, on the New Jersey shore, one comes to the town of Riverton. In 1865 the founding fathers of Riverton agreed that they would organize the first yacht club on the Delaware. They employed the Riverton Iron Pier for the purpose, which was also used by the sidewheel vessel that ferried passengers to and from Philadelphia. The club, dedicated in July of 1865, is still very much active with sailboat races, instruction for children, and regattas. Many world and national sailing champions have graduated from the yacht club's enthusiastic sailing program.

Dredge Harbor, on the New Jersey side of the river and about eight miles above the Ben Franklin Bridge, offers five marinas and a large selection of small-craft services and facilities. If at all possible, it would be a good idea to make advance reservations for dock space at these marinas, since they seldom monitor the VHF band. Public transportation to Philadelphia from Dredge Harbor, by either land or water taxi, is quick and easy. Contact the water taxi on

VHF Ch-68 or by calling (215) 351-4170. The marinas in Dredge Harbor are capable of supplying berths, fuel, supplies, haul-out, repairs, marine hardware, canvas work, and much more.

Dredge Harbor is also the home of the Cherubini Boat Company, which manufactures fiberglass sailboats and has the distinction of being the only fiberglass schooner manufacturer in the world. The schooner rig, which is seldom seen today, was once the rig of choice for much of America's coastal commerce until the early part of this century. I must admit to being prejudiced toward the schooner rig, as I consider it the prettiest sailing rig ever developed.

Just upriver from Dredge Harbor, on the New Jersey side of the river and about six miles north of Camden, one comes to the Rancocas Creek. It was named for the American Indian tribe that lived on its shores. The river originates in Lebanon State Forest and flows through high wooded shores to Mount Holly, where it changes to a low-land tidewater stream before joining the Delaware. This is a creek with deep water, where local boaters frequently anchor. If you decide to drop the hook here, be sure to stay out of the channel, since there is sand-and-gravel barge traffic as far as the first bridge. There are small-craft facilities on the north shore of the creek, just before the first bridge, as well as up river at Bridgeboro. From April 1 to October 1, the first bridge on the Rancocas

The Cherubini Boat Company at Dredge Harbor

between Riverside and Delanco, or Route-543 (with a vertical clearance of 4 feet), and the railroad bridge just beyond (with a vertical clearance of 3 feet), will open on demand from 7 A.M. to 11 P.M. Outside of these hours they will not open, and between November 1 and March 31, a twenty-four-hour notice must be given.

About four miles farther up the Delaware, on the Pennsylvania side, just beyond Neshaminy Creek, one will find a state marina. Although the marina welcomes transients, space can be very limited at the height of the season. Several more boatyards are located further up Neshaminy Creek, within three-quarters of a mile from its mouth.

The quaint town of Burlington, New Jersey, about seven miles beyond Dredge Harbor, was a bustling mercantile port presided over by Quaker businessmen 300 years ago. (In 1789, James Fenimore Cooper was born in a two-story stuccoed house on Main Street, which is now owned by the Burlington County Historical Society.) Now, Burlington resembles the quintessential small town at the turn of the century. Tours are provided through historic homes, and there are established parks along most of Burlington's Delaware River waterfront.

To the north of town the Delaware separates around Burlington Island, where the west side of the island is the main channel. Skippers of sailboats who are considering gunkholing around the east side should take note of the 45-foot power lines across the waterway.

On the east side of Burlington Island, about a half mile up and just beyond the Assiscunk Creek, one will find Curtin Marina, with docks and mooring buoys. It has a marine store, engine repair services, a canvas shop, and a restaurant overlooking the water.

Two miles north of Burlington Island, the Delaware takes a ninety degree turn to the east at Florence Bend. At this point we are about nine miles below the head of navigation at Trenton. The town of Florence is on the New Jersey shore, and across the river in Tullytown is Tullytown Cove, a basin about one thousand yards long, with a narrow entrance off the river. The entrance is about a quarter of a mile north of the large yellow fuel tank on the Pennsylvania shore. It is a locally popular anchorage, protected from the wash of river traffic. As a point of reference, there's a large park sloping down to the river in Florence, directly across the river from the entrance to Tullytown Cove.

Bordentown is about seven miles upriver from Florence Bend, on a high bank on the southeastern side of the entrance to Crosswicks Creek. It is one of central New Jersey's oldest settlements. In 1751 Joseph Borden, Jr. started the first weekly sailing packet line that provided a connection between Philadelphia and the New Jersey stagecoach line to Perth Amboy. Once at Perth

The entrance into Tullytown Cove

Amboy the passengers boarded a sailboat for the final leg of their journey to New York City. The trip from Philadelphia to New York took three days, considered breakneck speed at the time. Bordentown, the exchange point between stagecoach and sailboat, developed from this venture. In later years it became the terminus for another mode of transportation along the Delaware and Raritan Canal (discussed in chapter 2), which was closed in 1932.

The roster of Bordentown citizens includes such notables as Clara Barton, founder of the American Red Cross; Francis Hopkinson, a signer of the Declaration of Independence; and Joseph, the eldest brother of Napoleon Bonaparte. Joseph had been King of Naples and then King of Spain. When his brother's reign came to an end, he fled to America in disguise. He purchased more than one thousand acres of land near Bordentown, on a high hill overlooking the river, and named it Port Breeze. Only the land now exists, since the original buildings were destroyed by fire. During his fourteen years in Bordentown, Joseph contributed much to the community and was well liked.

In 1790, years before Fulton's much-publicized steamboat service on the Hudson River, John Fitch established a steamboat service on the Delaware between Bordentown, New Jersey, and Philadelphia. The steamboat ran on a regular schedule with few breakdowns, and the twenty-five mile trip could be made in four hours.

At Bordentown the river takes a ninety degree turn to the west, and the head of navigation at Trenton is only a few miles up river. Up Crosswicks Creek in Bordentown, just beyond the new highway bridge, two membership-only yacht clubs can be seen from the river.

About three miles north of Bordentown, Ross Marine Service can be found on the New Jersey shore about two miles south of Trenton. It is immediately north of the Public Service Electric and Gas Company complex, which is easily identified by the two tall chimneys. Ross Marine usually has slips for transients, with about 4 feet of water at low tide. From this location there is nothing within walking or easy biking distance.

Within view of the bridges at Trenton, that mark the end of our voyage up the Delaware, there is a high concrete bulkhead along the New Jersey shore that is listed on the chart as The Trenton Marine Terminal. It was used during World War II for loading heavy equipment aboard ships. The Trenton Marine Center is at the southern end of this bulkhead. It has a floating dock parallel to the shoreline in 25 to 30 feet of water, a boat-elevator on the face of the bulkhead for launching and retrieving small craft, engine repair services, parts, and a marine supply store. It frequently can provide an overnight berth for transients. At the north end of this same bulkhead there is a town park, where you'll see locals using long lines to fish down the vertical thirty-foot concrete face that rises from the river.

Along the final mile of the passage to the bridges at Trenton, be careful not to stray west of the marked channel; there are submerged rocks all along the Pennsylvania side of the river.

Washington Crossing is located seven miles north of Trenton. On Christmas night of 1776 Washington and his army, almost in rags, crossed the river in small boats to attack the Hessians. The towns on both sides of the river at that point, both in New Jersey and Pennsylvania, were named Washington Crossing. The event was immortalized by artist Emanuel Leutze in his famous painting. Most safety-conscious boaters, when looking at the painting of the small craft and ice-strewn river, think to themselves, "George, please sit down!"

Downstream from Washington's Crossing, and just north of the bridge in Trenton, there is a series of rapids, the Great Falls of the Delaware. Above the rapids the river is fresh, and below the rapids it's tidal and brackish. The tidal range at Trenton is nearly eight feet, the highest in New Jersey. Trenton is on a latitude just 12 nautical miles south of Sandy Hook, which is 42 miles away, across the narrow neck of New Jersey. To reach Sandy Hook by water is quite another matter; it's a trip of 260 miles. It is little wonder that the Delaware & Raritan Canal was so popular before it was replaced by the railroads and highways of today.

The head of navigation on the Delaware River at Trenton

At this spot the last navigational buoy (which is just south of the Amtrack railroad bridge that joins the capital of New Jersey with Pennsylvania) marks the head of navigation on the Delaware River. This buoy also marks the end of our cruise of New Jersey's navigable waterways. Although we've covered the major tide-water arteries, there are still hundreds of other side trips left to make—opportunities to explore and gunkhole on New Jersey's waters are boundless. Will I see you on the water?

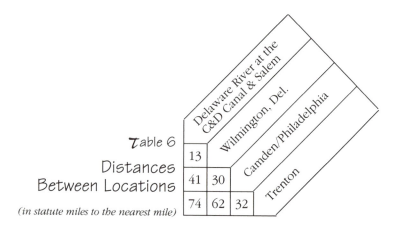

Table 6

Distances
Between Locations

(in statute miles to the nearest mile)

	Delaware River at the C&D Canal & Salem	Wilmington, Del.	Camden/Philadelphia	Trenton
	13			
	41	30		
	74	62	32	

General Information for Cruising

*T*he Responsibilities of the Skipper

It is the responsibility and duty of the skipper on a small boat to learn the job of being a skipper. Study, thought, and prudence are prerequisites, and until the skipper has gained enough experience, conservatism is the key. As the saying goes, "It is better to be an old sailor than a bold sailor."

The fate of those on the water depends on the type and condition of the vessel as well as on the crew. Just as with a chain, the weakest link determines its strength, regardless of the condition of the rest of the chain. So whenever preparing for a cruise in a small boat, there are certain prerequisites in both hardware and mental software. Some suggestions are:

1. Have up-to-date charts on board. Learn how to read them, and use them.
2. If the cruising plans include an offshore passage, alert someone on shore regarding the itinerary of the planned trip, along with expected times of arrival.
3. Brief the crew and passengers on safety gear before shoving off. Show them where life jackets and fire extinguishers are located and how to use them. Explain how to use the throwable flotation devices. Also determine if there are any nonswimmers on board. Establish rules for wearing life jackets for both nonswimmers and children.
4. Briefly explain man-overboard procedures. If everyone aboard, apart from the skipper, are relatively inexperienced, show the most knowledgeable how to stop the boat when under power or sail. Also explain, as simply as possible, how to make an emergency call on the VHF radio.
5. If aboard a sailboat, describe the special things to watch out for, including the results of an accidental jibe.
6. Check weather conditions before leaving, and again while out on the water.
7. Have prescribed safety equipment on board, including the correct number and size of life jackets for all passengers and crew members.
8. Have adequate anchors and anchor line.

9. Make sure the navigation lights are operational.
10. Be sure the fuel supply is adequate for the proposed trip.
11. If trailering to a launching ramp, check out the trailer, lights, safety chains, and bearings.
12. Know the height above water of the tallest part of the boat, so there is no indecision when approaching bridges. At all bridges, there are bridge-height boards fastened to the abutments bordering the navigable opening. The numbers at the water's surface indicate the actual clearance from water to bridge. Due to tides, wind, or rainfall, this is often different from the charted clearance.
13. Finally, abide by the rules of the road, and don't forget common courtesy.

Until a few years ago, getting help when your boat was disabled was as simple as calling the Coast Guard, but in the 1980s the policy of the Coast Guard was changed, with a mandate that nonemergency calls would not be handled by Coast Guard personnel. These nonemergency situations include running out of fuel, having engine problems, or running aground when there is no injury to people on board and the situation is not life threatening. The void in obtaining help in these situations has been filled by commercial towing companies, which now handle all nonemergency situations. Boaters asking for assistance (make a general call for a tow on Ch-16) should expect to pay more than $100 an hour from the time the towboat leaves the dock until it returns. This can make a weekend error in judgment rather expensive, since the average tow involves a two to three hour operation. To ease these unexpected contingencies, yearly towing insurance policies can be obtained, and some boating organizations include towing insurance as part of their membership fee.

Also, be aware that if a friendly boater offers to give you a tow for a small fee—it is illegal. Before one can accept money for towing, one is required to obtain a Coast Guard Towing License.

Safety on board is important in other ways, which are more personal but are serious nonetheless. When out on the water, sunburn is an all too common occurrence. Reflection from the water and the deck subjects the body to more sun intensity than one would be subjected to if on the beach. It is a good idea to keep a high-number sunscreen on board—one with both UVA and UVB inhibitors. We also keep a supply of wide-brimmed hats with tethers on board for those guests who have forgotten to bring their own.

It is always a good idea for the boat skipper to find out if anyone has a history of motion sickness. We keep Bonine and Dramamine on board, as well as acupressure wristbands, which many prefer and find effective. For extended periods on the water—many hours or several days at sea—the behind-the-ear Transderm Scop patch is very effective, but this requires a doctor's prescription.

Since all medications produce possible negative side effects, it is important that directions be read and understood. As an example, most people find that taking a small amount of alcohol, even many hours after a Bonine tablet, makes it almost impossible to stay awake. In the case of pregnant women, children, those with medical problems, and those on other medications, understanding the limitations of seasick remedies is especially important.

Before modern-day medications, ginger was the remedy for nausea. In fact, ginger-ale was developed as a cure for an upset stomach.

For some who are prone to mal-de-mer, keeping their eyes on the horizon and avoiding reading or going below is all that is necessary. Many others develop immunity after prolonged time on the water; while still others (including Britain's foremost seaman in the late eighteenth century, Admiral Horatio Nelson), get seasick whenever on board a boat.

Most important of all, it is the responsibility of the skipper to do his or her homework. When on a cruise or boat delivery, my nightly routine consists of going over the proposed route for the next day. Some of the things I check for are channel depths, bridge heights and opening times, potential storm anchorages, sources of fuel and supplies, and interesting and safe stop-over spots for the next night. I mark my charts with the appropriate notes, which not only is a great help the following day but a source of information for future cruises. We always keep a selection of navigational information on board, and I have included a list of suggested publications later in this chapter.

It is common for skippers who are about to start a voyage to a new area or on a new body of water to feel apprehensive. This is especially true for the novice who is about to begin an ocean passage for the first time. A little fear and anxiety is good. It keeps the adrenaline pumping and prompts preplanning and alertness. Too much fear can erode the skipper's abilities and ruin what would otherwise be an exciting voyage. Too little fear is also a bad sign; it fosters complacency. Desiderius Erasmus (1455?–1536), Dutch scholar and theologian, hit the nail on the head when he wrote: "Only the dolt showeth no fear."

Weather and Seasonal Changes on New Jersey Waters

Winter months produce the roughest seas along the New Jersey coast, with gales up to five percent of the time between November and March. In January, ocean waves of more than eight feet occur up to twenty-five percent of the time, and forty-foot waves have been recorded.

During many of New Jersey's winters, the Intracoastal Waterway, as well as the Delaware River, can freeze solid all the way across. The ice can drag buoys off-station and can destroy or incapacitate any of New Jersey's aids to navigation. By the end of many winters ten percent or more of the navigational aids are missing, damaged, off-station, extinguished, destroyed, or leaning, so that an early spring cruise becomes more chancy than one later in the season. In addition, winter storms may rearrange the bottom and create shoal spots across the waterway, usually near inlets. These spots may not have been dredged as yet, or buoys relocated.

With the arrival of spring, winds and waves become more subdued, as the

Our schooner, *Delphinus*, is anchored in a dense advection fog for 36 hours at Horseshoe Cove, inside Sandy Hook

semipermanent Bermuda high begins to dominate our weather. The possibility of advection fog increases significantly in the spring, especially on the northern coastal waters, as warm moist air flows across the still-cold water. May is statistically the worst month for fog, but we have frequently had our plans interrupted through late June.

Typical summer weather will include a couple of weeks of warm, humid days, with winds out of the south or southwest. During the daytime, along the intracoastal waters, a sea breeze develops about midday, and winds shift in from the ocean. This sea breeze can add to the prevailing winds and cause higher than forecasted winds on the inland waters and along the coast. On hot, humid days there is always the possibility of scattered thunderstorms, and from midsummer until October, there is a potential threat of tropical storms or hurricanes.

Fall weather typically consists of periods of dry sunny days and cool nights, and the threat of tropical storms begins to decrease. Radiation fog becomes more frequent, forming inland at night, then drifting toward coastal waters in the early morning. This type of fog is more local than are the advection fogs of spring, and it usually burns off by midday. The prevailing winds during September and October are from the northeast, a bonus for those sailboats heading south for the winter. From November to March prevailing winds are from the northwest.

Tides and Storms

Poets and ancient cultures have long compared life itself with the tides. Along the North Sea coast of England it was believed that most deaths occurred at ebb tide, as in, "life ebbs away with the tide." Historically, a flood tide has been considered an omen of good fortune, and an ebb tide has been considered foreboding.

Tides are created chiefly from the gravitational effects of the moon and the sun, as well as from atmospheric pressure. The wind is also an important factor, and is of great importance to our area. (I will say more about the wind later.) The moon is the major force in creating tides; its gravitational pull is about two and one quarter times that of the sun, so that our tides usually "follow the moon," but are slightly modified by the gravitation of the sun. The gravitational effects of the moon and sun generally create two high and two low tides every day.

The moon rotates around the earth so that it passes over the same longitude about once every twenty-four hours and fifty minutes. This means that at any given location, tides occur about fifty minutes later every day. If you see a high tide at 9 A.M. Monday morning, you can expect a high tide to occur at 9:50 A.M. Tuesday morning, at 10:40 A.M. Wednesday morning, and so on.

When the sun and the moon are in line with the earth, which happens at the time of a new moon or a full moon, the gravitational pull on the water is greater than average, and so-called *spring* tides occur. In this case, spring does not refer to the time of the year but rather to the the welling-up of the water, as from a spring. When the sun and moon are at right angles to the earth, with the moon in its first or third quarter, the gravitational pulls tend to cancel out slightly, and we have less than average, or *neap* tides.

The tides created by the gravitation of the sun and the moon are called celestial tides, as opposed to those tidal effects created by atmospheric pressure or the wind. Printed tide tables, as well as tide computer programs, allow the celestial tides to be calculated years in advance. One of the things these tables and programs can't show us, however, is the effect of atmospheric pressure and wind on the tides—and the wind effects are of great importance to the residents and mariners of the New Jersey shoreline.

Those cruising New Jersey's inland tidal waters, protected by barrier islands, know that the tides there are considerably less than those on the ocean side of the barrier islands. This is due to the narrow inlets that limit the exchange of water between ocean and bay. This limited water exchange causes low tides in the bay that are actually higher than those in the ocean, and high tides in the bay that are actually lower than those in the ocean. At high tide, the ocean tries to fill up the bay, but before it gets a chance, the tide has changed and begun to drop; so that tide variations in the bay never approach those on the ocean side of the island. This also causes the times of high and low tides in the bays to lag behind those for the ocean.

Many boaters along our Atlantic coastline think it would be great if the inlets to the ocean were broad and deep—in actuality this would be a disaster.

If there were no longer a restriction of water flow between the ocean and the bay, high and low tides in the bay would be the same as those in the ocean. At low tide a large percentage of the bottom of the Intracoastal Waterway would be exposed, and most of the recreational activities on the water, not to mention much of the bay's ecology, would cease to exist. High tides in the bays, with water levels the same as in the ocean, would create flooding comparable to that of a nor'easter or a hurricane. Under these conditions people would not be able to live on most of the barrier islands or on the mainland side of the bays. So when people complain about our inlets, I say, "I'll take them just as they are, thank you very much!"

But why do nor'easters seem to cause trouble for those barrier islands and inland bays, even more so than hurricanes; and why then don't the narrow inlets protect the bays?

During an extended blow, such as the nor'easters of 1962, 1991, 1992, and 1993, a different scenario takes place. During a long blow (twelve hours or more) an ocean current is produced by the wind. The rule of thumb is that this current is about two percent of the wind speed, so that during an extended blow of 60 mph toward our shore, a current of 1.2 mph is set up. This current is directed to the whole coastline and causes the water to mound up against the shore, creating higher than predicted tides. This mounding effect is very real, with the ocean water level along the shore much higher than it is many miles out to sea. On top of this mound of water are the unusually high wind-created waves. The height of these waves is directly related to the wind speed, its duration, and the distance that these winds are blowing across the water, or the fetch. During the 1962 storm, the fetch was more than 1,000 miles.

During a nor'easter, the storm surge created by the winds and the current forces ocean waters into the inlets; even during celestial low tide, the height of the ocean water, along with the wind, does not allow water to escape from the bays. The next ocean high tide again adds water to the bays until, after a series of high tides, the water level in the bays approaches that of high tide in the ocean.

The American Red Cross estimates that more than 10,000 homes in New Jersey were either destroyed or damaged during the December 1992 nor'easter. Many old-timers say it was the worst storm they've seen since the 1938 hurricane, and that didn't last as long. We are fortunate that most of the hurricanes that have visited this area have been rapid travelers. In a hurricane, the low pressure in the eye can suck up the ocean into unusually high tides, much as soda is sucked up by a straw. As it approaches us from the south, its on shore winds can replicate the effects of a nor'easter. Fortunately, hurricanes at this latitude pass by rapidly, so that the piling up of the water against our coast is reduced—and remember, it usually takes more than one high tide to fill up the bays. As the eye passes by us, there is a wind shift, and water is blown out of the bays. The tidal effects of the wind on the inland tidewaters is commonly called blow-in and blow-out tides. They are a major cause of the varying tide heights in the bays, even greater than the effects of the moon and the sun.

National Weather Service officials characterized the December 1992 nor'easter as a one-hundred-year storm. Others dubbed it the storm of the century. Three months later the appellation was repeated and applied to the March 13 storm, along with the added distinction of "the white hurricane." This was an appropriate name, since in many ways the March storm resembled a hurricane more than it did a typical nor'easter. Satellite photographs even revealed an eye.

Let's hope that the latest one-hundred-year storm holds on to its title and receives no further challenges.

The VHF-FM Marine Band

The two-way VHF-FM marine radio is an important accessory for the recreational boater. These radios are available as either fixed-mount or hand-held units. A station license is required (applications forms are included with purchase). It is important that the required license be obtained. Recent Coast Guard boardings of boats—usually for an unrelated reason—have resulted in sizable fines when an unlicensed VHF-FM marine radio was found on board. Fines of $1,000 or more are not uncommon.

Channel 16 (Ch-16) is the international distress, urgency, safety, calling, and reply frequency for vessels and coastal stations. In 1992, in order to relieve congestion on Ch-16, the FCC designated Channel 9 as the general-purpose calling frequency for recreational boats. This is still considered a recommendation, not a requirement. Recreational boats should still make emergency and safety calls on Ch-16.

After an initial contact via Ch-9 or Ch-16, the balance of the contact must be made on another appropriate channel. For example, the Coast Guard may request that one change to Channel 22A. When the letter A is added to the channel number, it indicates that this channel frequency is a frequency used in the U.S. and one that is different from the international channel frequency. When changing to a channel designated with an A, make sure the VHF radio is switched to USA and not International. It is easy to remember that A means American frequency.

Bridge operators monitor Ch-13 and Ch-16, and they also respond to the usual "one long, one short" horn signal. They are generally prompt and cooperative. Many bridges have restricted opening hours. When a call is made for an opening and the bridge operator is unable to comply, he or she will explain the schedule using Ch-13. A bridge-opening request should be made on low power (1-watt), with the name or location of the bridge given in the call.

Another important thing to make note of is the list of VHF-FM weather channels that are available on New Jersey waters:

New York City	WX-1
Atlantic City	WX-2
Lewes, Delaware	WX-1
Philadelphia	WX-3

When one makes phone calls on VHF-FM, the Public Coast Marine Operators (from north to south) are on

New York City, N.Y.	25, 26, 28, 84, 86
Navesink, N.J. (south of Sandy Hook)	24
Manasquan, N.J.	85
Bayville, N.J. (south of Toms River)	27
Beach Haven, N.J. (north of Atlantic City)	25
Atlantic City, N.J. (Ventnor)	87
Sea Isle City, N.J. (north of Cape May)	26
Cape May, N.J.	24
Lewes, Del. (Cape Henlopen)	27
Philadelphia, Pa.	26, 85

*C*ellular Phones and Distress Calls to the Coast Guard

Skippers with cellular phones on board have a special emergency code for contacting the Coast Guard. The call, which is free of charge, connects the boater to either the Sandy Hook Station, when calls are made from north of Toms River, or the Cape May Station, when calls are made from south of Toms River. The service, which has been available for more than four years, can be accessed by dialing: *CG.

Although a typical portable cellular phone has an output of about .6 watts and a limited range, cellular phones with a 3-watt output (such as car phones), along with a marine antenna, have ranges of up to forty or fifty miles.

One advantage of having a cellular phone over using VHF-FM is the relative privacy it offers—but this privacy adds a negative feature when the phone is used for an emergency at sea. With VHF-FM, there may be other boats nearby that can hear the distress call and come to one's aid; this is not so when one uses a cellular phone. Also, during a rescue mission in which boats or helicopters are used, communication directly to them is impossible with a cellular phone, whereas, it is possible if one is using VHF.

*C*harts

Throughout the book I've tried to emphasize the importance of up-to-date charts. Nautical charts, at first glance, can be a little intimidating, and they require some study before the navigator feels comfortable using them. NOAA publishes a booklet entitled "Chart No. 1," which provides all the symbols used on nautical charts; this should be kept on board with one's other charts. Frequently, some, but not necessarily all, of the abbreviations used on the charts can be found in a small table somewhere on the chart itself.

Charts come in a variety of formats and sizes, and they use several different types of measuring systems. Intracoastal charts measure distances in statute miles; water depths in feet, measured at average low tide; and bridge clearances in feet, measured at average high tide. Other charts may use nautical miles or fathoms, so it is important to check the key for your chart.

The Mapping Agency in Washington, D.C., has established a number system for charts, which is broken up into geographical areas. For the northeast coast, the chart numbers range from 12,000 to 13,000. For example, one will find that Sandy Hook to Little Egg Harbor is chart #12324.

Every chart also shows the date of issue so that out-of-date charts can be identified and discarded.

The charts that cover New Jersey's coastal and inland waters are

Yonkers to Piermont	#12346
(the Hudson River at the N.J.-N.Y. state line)	
George Washington Bridge to Yonkers	#12345
(the Hudson River south to the G.W. Bridge)	
Day's Point to George Washington Bridge	#12341
(the Hudson River south to Weehawkin)	
Hudson and East Rivers—Governor's Island to 67th Street	#12335
(Lower Manhattan)	
New York Harbor—Upper Bay & Narrows-Anchorage Chart	#12334
(N.Y.'s Upper Bay to south of the Verrazano Bridge)	
New York Lower Bay—Northern Part	#12402
Raritan Bay and Southern Part of Arthur Kill	#12331
Kill Van Kull and Northern Arthur Kill	#12333
Raritan River, Raritan Bay to New Brunswick	#12332
Intracoastal Waterway—Sandy Hook to Little Egg Harbor	#12324
Intracoastal Waterway—Little Egg Harbor to Cape May	#12316
Delaware Bay	#12304
Delaware River—Smyrna River to Wilmington	#12311
Wilmington to Philadelphia	#12312
Philadelphia to Trenton	#12314

Note: A single chart, numbered 12327, covers the same area as the charts listed above numbered 12335, 12334, 12402, 12331, and 12333, but with less detail.

Sales agents for charts, *Tide Tables, Tidal Current Diagrams, Tidal Charts,* and *Coast Pilots* can be found at some marine-supply stores, boat yards, and marinas. A list of authorized sales agents and chart catalogs is available, for free, upon request from:

National Ocean Service
Distribution Branch (N/CG33)
6501 Lafayette Ave.
Riverdale, Md. 20737

Charts and chart books are also available from private publishers, such as: Waterway Guide; BBA; Embassy Coastal Cruising; Home Port Chart, Inc.; Boating Almanac; and several others.

In the last few years electronic chart displays have become a practical alternative for many boaters. These digital charts are displayed on an electronic screen. Navigational information comes from chart data cartridges, each storing from six to ninety charts, that are based on NOAA charts. In addition, this system can be coupled with an on-board GPS or Loran that will insert the boat's position directly onto the screen's chart display. Way points can be indicated by pointing to the desired location, thus eliminating data-entry errors.

No universal format has yet been established for electronic chart systems, so there are several incompatible systems. The two major systems are C-Map and Navionics, which have the major share of the market. Each C-Map cartridge contains about six to ten charts, at a cost of about $150, while Navionics cartridges contain up to ninety charts, at a cost of between $149 and $395.

Currently, there are also chart programs that can be run on a home desktop or laptop computer, providing the unit has a 286 or higher processor, a hard disk, a VGA graphics adapter, and a VGA display. Charts are available on 3.5″ floppy disks or on CD-ROM.

The system choice for any of the electronic charts will determine the hardware, and there are a wide range of presentations and accessories, depending on the system selected.

Electronic charts do not have nearly the detail of information as do printed charts, and changes of such things as buoy numbers and locations can require the purchase of a new disk, cartridge, or tape (or in some cases may be made by software changes directly to the user's database). If electronic charts are used, the skipper must remember that a power-source failure, an electronic failure due to moisture or hardware malfunction, or a nearby lightning strike can leave the boat without a chart unless paper charts are also on board.

Since the electronic segment of the boating industry is progressing in leaps and bounds, this profile of the current electronic chart capabilities and limitations are just that—current as of this writing. Those contemplating the purchase of an electronic chart system should research the latest units and programs available.

As with nearly every system on recreational craft, backup, or redundancy, is always important, and the prudent skipper who uses an electronic chart system on board should also invest in hard-copy charts.

Navigational Instruments
The Compass

Since the days when ancient navigators first floated bits of lodestone or of magnetized iron on pieces of cork in a bowl of water, the compass has been the primary tool for navigation. Its basic construction changed little—until this century. More than fifty years ago the gyrocompass made its debut and, more recently, the electronic *fluxgate* compass, with digital or analog liquid-crystal display, has taken its place as the latest advancement in compass technology. This new style of compass allows for large, easily read numbers; off-course indicators that utilize bar graphs, remote-display capability, automatic deviation correction, and many other features.

RDF

The RDF, or Radio Direction Finder, was one of the first electronic navigation systems used aboard small boats. It utilized broadcast stations or low frequency radio shore stations (radio beacons) to determine lines of position and to triangulate their location. Today, the more sophisticated electronic systems have usurped it, and RDF has become a kind of dinosaur. Few boats have RDFs on board, and there are even fewer manufacturers. RDF radio beacons in New Jersey were located at the inlets of Manasquan, Barnegat, Atlantic City, and Cape May. Although they can be found on the latest charts, all four beacons were recently discontinued.

Radar

Radio Detecting And Ranging is better known by its acronym RADAR, and has been in practical use since World War II. The first experiments were made by Guglielmo Marconi, the father of radio. The system determines distances and azimuths from transmitted pulses of high-frequency radio signals that are then reflected by so-called targets—other boats, buoys, land masses, buildings, bridges, and so on, or by *transponders,* which initiate their own radar signal when prompted by another radar. The same antenna is used for the transmit and receive pulses, and the time it takes for the signal to make the round trip is timed and used for the screen display.

In recent years, small-craft radars have been considerably reduced in size, power requirements, and price, while expanding their on-screen programs and interface capabilities. Now, most units use LCD screens (liquid crystal display), which replace the more cumbersome and power-hungry CRTs (cathode ray tubes) of the past. All modern units now use raster display (just like your TV set) rather than the rotating display of previous years. This greatly improves the ease of operation. The ability of a radar unit to network with other electronic gear on board, such as Loran, autopilot, GPS, or electronic charts, is an important consideration when one is purchasing a new one. The type of antenna, the beam width, the range, and the antenna placement are also important concerns that should be discussed before the purchase is made and the installation completed.

Loran-C

LORAN, an acronym for Long Range Navigation, has until recently been the system of choice for determining a small boat's position in coastal waters. Now a relatively new system, GPS, the satellite Global Position System, has begun to attract the small-boat market as its price has dropped nearly as low as the price of Loran. During the Radionavigation Users Conference in 1993, the Commander of the U.S. Coast Guard suggested that, due to the success of the GPS system, it would be technically and economically justified to terminate

Loran-C by the year 2000. Since then, there have been indications that the termi-nation date might be even sooner. The Defense Department stopped using Loran in 1994, and the U.S. Coast Guard has begun using the new DGPS system as its primary positioning system.

According to BOAT/US, there are between 800,000 and 1 million Loran-C receivers in use in the U.S. at the present time. The Coast Guard estimates it could save $25 million a year by discontinuing the operation.

The Loran receiver develops its fixes from powerful low-frequency land-based transmitters scattered along the coast as well as inland. By measuring the time differences of the signals received from these stations (TDs) the units give readouts either of these TD lines (shown on most charts) or of latitude and longitude. Since the TD lines are hyperbolas, the system is called a hyperbolic navigational system.

GPS and DGPS

Satellite navigation began in the mid 1960s with the U.S. Navy's NAV-SAT system (Navy Satellite). It is based on the Doppler-shift phenomenon, the apparent change in wavelengths as the distance between the source and the receiving station is increasing or decreasing. This is the same effect that is heard when a car horn or a train whistle changes from a higher to a lower pitch as it goes by.

The second generation satellite navigation system, the one now available to recreational boaters, is known as the NAVSTAR Global Positioning System, or simply GPS. The GPS receiver monitors signals from U.S. Air Force satellites (twenty-six at the time of this writing) located 10,898 miles above the earth, in polar orbits. It takes three of these satellites to provide a two-dimensional fix (latitude and longitude), and four to provide three dimensions, including alti-tude. The GPS receivers display position, usually within one-hundred meters or closer, on LCDs. Hand-held units are available with built-in antennas, and per-manently mounted units have external antennas. The GPS receivers come with a wide range of options in power requirements, software, and their ability to interface with other electronic equipment on board. They frequently display ten, twenty, or more pages of navigational information. Some GPS units have differential capability, which means that with the addition of another separate receiver to monitor special land-based AM stations, the GPS position accuracy can be displayed to within five to ten meters. This differential capability is not available far out at sea or in certain coastal areas of the United States. Many of these land stations are in the process of being constructed or are still on the drawing boards. The official target date for the DGPS system to become opera-tional is 1996. Current status of the differential GPS transmitters (DGPS) can be obtained from the Coast Guard GPS Information Center at (703) 313-5900, or from their computer bulletin board service at (703) 313-5900.

Networking of Navigational Equipment

When electronic navigational equipment first began proliferating on small boats, the individual systems had no way of exchanging information. Early equipment manufacturers, lacking universal interface language, developed languages within each company to tie equipment together. This lack of a universal electronic language was bad for consumers, since it prevented mixing equipment from different manufacturers. Finally, in 1979, the National Marine Electronics Association (NMEA) began drafting an interface protocol, and in 1980 the NMEA 0180 format was adopted.

The NMEA 0180 was a relatively simplistic system, and the rapid progression of marine electronics required more flexibility—which was provided by the NMEA 0183 format (adopted in 1983) that went on to become an international standard. But even this system did not provide a language adaptable enough for the rapid growth in marine electronics, and once again manufacturers began solving the problem with individual proprietary systems.

The NMEA is now developing a format that will allow several different electronic navigational systems to share the same line and to exchange information at the same time. This new protocol, as yet unnumbered, should be promulgated by early 1996. So, let this be a caveat for the consumer—when purchasing new equipment, determine interface formats and interconnection possibilities.

*M*arine Sanitation Devices

With the increased population density near our coastal waters as well as the burgeoning boating population that uses these waters, sewage disposal, both along the shore and on the water, has become critical. The regulations governing sewage discharge from boats went into effect in 1980 and have not changed appreciably since then. Basically, the law says that if a vessel has an installed head (a porta-potty is not an installed head), it must have an operable Coast Guard certified marine sanitation device (MSD). There are three types of MSDs. Types I and II macerate sewage and treat it with disinfectant chemicals, after which it can be pumped overboard. Type III is the no-discharge type, usually employing a holding tank, which must be pumped out at an on-shore pump-out station.

Many experts in the field believe that by 1997 most of the coastal states will be declared no-discharge areas (MSD Type III only) with the entire continental U.S. converting by the end of the century. There may be a grandfather clause for MSD Types I and II.

*R*eference Material

Although navigational equipment and charts provide a boater's basic requirements, there are many other sources of information available to the recreational boater, both in print as well as in less traditional formats.

Waterway Guide is a yearly publication that gives a detailed description of small-craft marinas (and their services) along the Intracoastal Waterway from Canada to the Mexican border. It is published in several editions. The *Waterway Guide, Northern Edition* covers New Jersey's waters as well as the coastal and intracoastal waters between the Canadian border and the Delmarva Peninsula.

Navigation Rules is published by the Coast Guard and details the rules of the road in both text and pictorial displays. It is "must" reading and should be kept on board as a reference.

The United States Coast Pilot is a government publication primarily designed for the commercial and professional seafarer. It is published in several editions. Edition #2 covers the Atlantic Coast from Cape Cod to Sandy Hook, including New York Harbor and the Hudson River. Edition #3 covers Sandy Hook to Cape Henry. These publications contain a wealth of information, including opening schedules for all bridges, and it contains an appendix of statistical information, time and distance, conversion tables, weather, and more. Since it is a government publication, it is all business.

Chapman's Piloting, Seamanship, and Small Boat Handling has been the bible of the recreational boater since 1922, and it is now in its sixty-first edition. The encyclopedic information it contains on every phase of small boat handling and navigation makes it an important learning text and reference.

Notice to Mariners is a weekly Coast Guard publication that gives the latest changes, additions, or deletions to aids-to-navigation, as well as information concerning potential hazards and any changes in the laws governing small craft. Each Coast Guard district publishes its own weekly *Notice to Mariners*, giving information for that district. The publication is free and can be obtained by contacting the appropriate district.

The First Coast Guard District covers the east coast from Eastport, Maine, to Toms River, New Jersey. Its *Notice to Mariners* can be obtained by contacting:

Commander, First Coast Guard District (oan)
408 Atlantic Avenue
Boston, Mass. 02110
1-800-848-3942, ext. 8338
FAX: (617) 223-8073

The Fifth Coast Guard District covers New Jersey's waters from Toms River, south. Its *Notice to Mariners* can be obtained by contacting:

Commander, Fifth Coast Guard District
Aids to Navigation Branch
Federal Building, 431 Crawford Street
Portsmouth, Va. 23704

(804) 398-6223
FAX: (804) 398-6303

The *Local Notice to Mariners,* as well as other marine information, is available on an electronic bulletin board service from the Global Positioning System Information Center, at 703-313-5910 (to receive information, 300-14,400 baud, 8-bit data required, no parity, 1 stop bit).

U.S. Coast Guard Light List is a government publication that features comprehensive, up-to-date, easy-to-follow listings of lights, buoys, sound signals, daybeacons, RACONS, radio beacons, and other aids to navigation maintained by or under the authority of the U.S. Coast Guard. The publication includes illustrations of aids to navigation and a glossary of terminology relating to these aids. Separate volumes are printed for each geographical area and may be obtained from the Superintendent of Documents, U.S. Government Printing Office, or from dealers of government charts.

These are just a few of the myriad publications and electronic information services available. Depending on the cruise intended, other periodicals to consider might include *Tide and Current Tables, Coastal Loran Coordinates,* and *Eldridge.* In recent years there have also been a large number of videos available, covering all topics from marine engine repair to "cruising into the sunset," which many people find appealing.

Computer Networks

As the information superhighway becomes a reality, those with computers now have the opportunity of obtaining recreational boating information through a variety of public and private computer networks.

Sea-Net is one of the services available to those who have a computer, a modem, and a communications software program that uses ANSI or VT-100. Sea-Net can be reached through a personal computer by dialing 1-719-687-7222. When the first screen comes up, type NEW, and Sea-Net will guide you through the initial sign on procedure. From the database you select a category and then move through subcategories to access the specific information of interest.

The Coast Guard Boating Safety Hotline is a 1-800 telephone number, in service weekdays, from 8 A.M. to 8 P.M. Eastern time. The Coast Guard has trained operators available to answer questions regarding rules and regulations, charts, boat-building, jet skis, hurricanes, Coast Guard boardings, and much more. This number can also be used to report a defect in a boat or equipment or to learn if a particular boat or item has been recalled or has been the subject of frequent complaints. Call 1-800-368-5647. This number should not be used to report a marine emergency or to request assistance on the water.

The Boat/U.S. Foundation Courseline is a 1-800 telephone number listing free courses in all phases of recreational boating. The computerized system lists more than 18,000 course locations nationwide. The 1-800-336-BOAT number is in service from 8 A.M. to 7 P.M. Eastern time.

Finally, there are many instructional programs available on floppy disks, including navigation, radar training, boat handling, rules-of-the-road, and so on.

To obtain further sources of information, I suggest browsing through book stores, marine stores, nautical catalogs, and the library.

⚓ Index

When the state name is not included in the listing, the location is in New Jersey.

Cherry Island Range, 173
Cherubini Boat Co., 105, 186
Chesapeake Bay, 17, 120, 127, 129, 165, 167
Chesapeake and Delaware Canal: chart of, 168; distances to and from, 148, 159, 163, 165, 169, 190; history of, 167; photograph of, 167; waterways to and

Chester, Penn., 175
China, 17–18
Christina River, Del., 175
Circle Line Ferry, 12
Clam Creek Basin, 109–110
Clamtown. See Tuckerton
Clarks Landing Marina, 60
Clean Ocean Action, 32
Clinton, President Bill, 157
Clyde A. Phillips, the, 158
Coast Guard (U.S.), 16, 35
Cohansey River, 154, 159–163
Cold Spring Harbor Inlet. See Cape May Inlet
Columbus, Christopher, 17
Commodore Bay Marina, 118
compass, 200
Compton Creek, 43–44
Conklin Island, 94
Constitution, the USS, 136
Cooper, James Fenimore, 37, 187
Cornell Harbor, 118
Corsons Inlet, 118, 142
Corsons Inlet State Park, 116
Cranberry Inlet, 70
Cross Ledge Shoal, 154
Crosswicks Creek, 187, 189
Cumberland County, 42, 120, 159
Curtin Marina, 187

Deepwater Point Range, 173
De Halve Maen. See Half Moon
Delanco, 187
Delaware, state of, 164–166, 173
Delaware and Raritan Canal, 50–51, 188–189
Delaware and Raritan Canal State Park, 51
Delaware Bay: chart of, 146; distances on, 165; ecology of, 148–149, 155, 157; history of, 17, 123–124, 149–150, 154, 157–160; on shore along, 125; photographs of, 150, 154–155, 160, 164; pi-

rates on, 167; State Marina at Fortescue 42; transiting, 67, 148–149, 153–154, 157, 159, 163–165, 173; waterways to and from, 120, 127, 129, 137, 145, 147, 150; weather on, 153, 157
Delaware City, Del., 169–170
Delaware City Branch Channel, 169
Delaware City Marina, 169
Delaware River: charts of, 168, 181; distances on, 190; ecology of, 69, 166, 176–178; history of, 19, 50–51, 74, 123, 149, 163, 166–167, 169–170, 173, 176–177, 184–189; navigation on, 154, 169–170, 173, 175–177, 179–187, 189–190; waterways to and from, 165, 167
Delaware Riverkeeper, 177
Delaware River Memorial Bridge, 173
Delaware State Park System, Del., 169, 175
Delmarva Peninsula, 97, 120, 127, 149
Delphinus, the, 4, 53, 194
Delran, 105
Department of Environmental Protection, 38
Department of the Interior, the, 107
Department of Transportation, 59
Dewey, Commodore, 177, 180
DGPS. See GPS
distress calls, 198
Doc's Place Restaurant, 94
Donitz, Admiral Karl, 30
Dorset Avenue bridge, 115
Double Creek Channel, 94
Dredge Harbor, 185, 187
Dunks Shoal, 159, 163

Earle Ammunition Pier. See Navy Pier, Raritan Bay
Earl of Bellomont. See Bellomont, Earl of
Easton, Penn., 19
East Point Lighthouse, 157
East River, N.Y., 15–16
ecology: Atlantic Ocean, 132–133; Barnegat Bay, 80, 83, 89; Belford Harbor, 43; Delaware Bay, 148–149, 155, 157; Delaware River, 176–177; Forsythe National Wildlife Refuge, 106–108; Greater NJ/NY Harbor, 32–34; Hackensack River, 21; Hudson River, 7–8; Kill Van Kull and Arthur Kill, 18–19; Navesink River, 38, 40; Pine Barrens, 68–69;

Ventnor, 116, 140
Ventnor Heights, 115
Verrazano, Giovanni da, 17, 97
Verrazano Bridge, N.Y., 16–18, 23, 31–32, 52
VHF-FM Marine Band, 197–198; Atlantic City marinas and, 109–110; bridges and, 65–66, 185; Camden/Philadelphia marinas and water taxi and, 179–180, 184–185; Cape May marinas and, 120, 127; C&D Canal and, 169; commercial traffic and, 7, 175; Hudson River marinas and, 10; Ocean City marinas and, 116; weather and, 53, 116, 196
Victoria Foundation, 83
Victory Bridge, 50
Viking Yacht Company, 104–105

Wading River, 105–106
Walt Whitman Bridge, 177
Waretown, 81, 90, 94
Washington, George, 189
Washington Canal, 50
Washington Crossing, N.J. and Penn., 189
Washington, D.C., 111
Water's Edge Restaurant, 78
Watershed Association of the Delaware River, 177
Wavertree, the, 15
weather, 53, 131, 193–194

weather channels on VHF-FM marine band, 197
Weehawken, 10
Weekstown, 105
Wehrlen Marina, 68
Welcome, the, 166
Westchester, N.Y., 6
Wetlands Institute, 118–119
Wharfside Restaurant, 60
Whitman, Walt, 184–185
Wiggins Park Camden County Marina, 182–183
Wildwood, 119–120, 132, 143–144
Wildwood Crest, 119–120
Willner, Andrew, 32–33
Wilmington, Del., 175, 190
wind, 6–7, 31, 80, 132, 143, 153, 175–176
Windows on the Bay Restaurant, 78
Woody's Sea Store, 75
World Trade Center, N.Y., 15
World Wars I and II: Cape May, 124–125; Donitz, Karl, 30; ICW, 64; Island Beach, 78; Narrows, the, 30–31; New Jersey coast, 30–31; Pea Patch Island, 173; Point Pleasant Canal, 61; Philadelphia, 176–177; Sandy Hook, 34–35; Trenton, 189; Tuckerton, 101

Yonkers, N.Y., 8

Zipf, Cindy, 32

About the Author

Captain Don Launer is a lifetime resident of New Jersey. He now lives in Forked River, on the shore of Barnegat Bay, on the state's central Atlantic coastline. He has held a U.S. Coast Guard captain's license for more than seventeen years and is a frequent contributor to boating magazines and newspapers, most notably *Cruising World* magazine, *Offshore* magazine, *SAIL* magazine, and the Jersey shore newspaper *The Beachcomber*. He is also northeast field-editor for the yearly publication *Waterway Guide*.

Over the years he has cruised New Jersey's waters extensively, while on vacation and while doing boat deliveries. He has also cruised the entire east coast from Canada to the Florida Keys, and he has skippered charters in the Bahamas, the Virgin Islands, and the Mediterranean. In what he likes to call his "previous life," he worked in commercial television, at ABC-TV in New York City, traveling the world to cover the Olympic Games. His work won him two Emmy Awards.

In addition to his captain's license, Don holds a General Class FCC license, the highest of the commercial radio licenses; an Amatuer Radio Operator's license; and a private pilot's license for both land and sea.

As a member of the Barnegat Baywatch program, he does water-quality monitoring of Barnegat Bay's waters twice a month during the boating season.

Don has been on or around the water all his life. As a child he spent his summers in Lavalette, on the New Jersey shore, or camping along the upper Delaware River, where his brother, Philip, and he would explore the waters in a variety of small craft.

Before World War II his family frequently spent summers in Europe. These shipboard crossings of the Atlantic, along with those he took when in the armed forces during the war, combine to make a dozen.

His earliest memory as a child took place on the water—during a nearly disastrous experience.

When he was about five years old, his mother was returning from Europe with him and his brother. A couple of days before arriving in New York City, the ship blundered into a late-summer hurricane that was moving rapidly up the coast. At that time hurricanes could not be tracked or forecast. Portholes were smashed, and at each roll of the ship, water poured through them. In their cabin, water was two or three feet deep. Their mother tied them into the upper bunk. The ship almost didn't make it, and when it arrived in New York, there was a long line of ambulances waiting for the passengers with broken bones and head injuries.

It didn't seem to dampen Don's enthusiasm for being on the water. He's owned his own boat since he was eleven years old, and has frequently had more than one at a time. He owns eight at this writing, and he's owned more than eighteen during his lifetime. Many of them he built himself.

He met his wife, Elsie, in the 1940s while he was working as a lifeguard. They have two children, and the entire family loves the water. Don's daughter, Kathy, wind-surfs and enjoys going out on her father's schooner—especially when small-craft warnings are up.

Kathy has carried the tradition to her own family. She taught her two daughters, Jennifer and Nancy, to swim before they could walk. They're completely at home in and around the water.

Don's son, Tom, owns a *Laser* sailboat and also enjoys his father's schooner, which he helped him build. Tom has been sailing with his father since he was two years old, and he had his own boat when he was four.

Now retired, Captain Launer cruises the East Coast in his two-masted schooner *Delphinus* and gunkholes in his Boston Whaler or his kayak.